Renegotiate
Your
Marriage

Renegotiate Your Marriage

Balance the Terms of Your Relationship as It Changes

A Couple's Guide to
Adapting to: Job Loss, Birth of a Child,
Moving, Empty Nest Syndrome, Infidelity,
Change in Income, and More of Life's Transitions

Bonnie Jacobson, PhD

Avon, Massachusetts

Published by
Adams Media, a division of F+W Media, Inc.
57 Littlefield Street, Avon, MA 02322. U.S.A.
www.adamsmedia.com

ISBN 10: 1-4405-2793-8
ISBN 13: 978-1-4405-2793-7
eISBN 10: 1-4405-2891-8
eISBN 13: 978-1-4405-2891-0

Printed in the United States of America.

10   9   8   7   6   5   4   3   2   1

Library of Congress Cataloging-in-Publication Data
is available from the publisher.

This publication is designed to provide accurate and authoritative information with regard to the subject matter covered. It is sold with the understanding that the publisher is not engaged in rendering legal, accounting,
or other professional advice. If legal advice or other expert assistance is
required, the services of a competent professional person should be sought.
—From a *Declaration of Principles* jointly adopted
by a Committee of the American Bar Association
and a Committee of Publishers and Associations

Many of the designations used by manufacturers and sellers to distinguish
their product are claimed as trademarks. Where those designations appear
in this book and Adams Media was aware of a trademark claim, the designations have been printed with initial capital letters.

This book is available at quantity discounts for bulk purchases.
For information, please call 1-800-289-0963.

To my inspirational bookends:

Rose (age 90) . . . . Ramona (age 5) and Ada Lu (age 3)

Acknowledgments

Where to start? Many thanks to all who have inspired me, especially Stephanie Abou, my incredible agent, and Paula Munier, the editor-in-chief of Adams Media who always supports and encourages me and asks for the moon. I love it because it forces me to try for the impossible. It's also been a pleasure to work with Stephanie Land, my writing partner. She is a magician, a speed maven, and a great, great writer.

I have many friends, colleagues, and family members who have offered exceptional advice and feedback on this project; Dr. Linda Carter is a negotiation genius—my only regret is not having gotten her involved sooner; Dr. Myrna Weissman is an undaunted, indomitable ally and perhaps the most competent person I know. She has taught me so much, especially on the subject of how people confront dying and death; Margot Weinshel offered invaluable insight and expertise about the common struggles faced by couples facing infertility. Suzanne Stutman—my sister, my colleague, my friend—is always there for advice and wisdom; Brad, who inspired me once again to write from my heart about renegotiation; and finally, Arie, who sits through each and every chapter and offers me uncensored and often entertaining feedback.

Yet another person whose influence can be felt in this book is Rose, an expert on living life to the fullest. Also Debra Ganz, my research assistant, who could not be more knowledgeable about how to find what and where almost instantly.

Dr. Bonnie Maslin is the reason I began to write. She is my friend, my mentor, my colleague. She inspires me with her uncompromising standards and capacity for treating patients with dignity. It seems for the last twenty-five years our lives have been on parallel tracks and I am grateful for our mutual support system.

Of course, this book could not have been written had my patients not provided me with such a privileged position in their lives. I am lucky to work with so many people who are wise, brilliant, open to change, and who have so much to teach me.

I give them my unconditional positive regard; they give me their trust and love. What a wonderful opportunity for all of us.

Thank you, my gratitude spills over.

Bonnie Jacobson

Contents

Part 3: Renegotiating How to Cherish One Another

Introduction

"People change and forget to tell us."

—LILLIAN HELLMAN

In 1970, archeologists working in Iraq discovered a piece of parchment dating from more than 2,500 years ago, which documented how a young couple, Tamut and Ananiah, negotiated a mutually acceptable marriage contract. Like the formal contracts that are still used in many strict religious communities and tradition-bound countries today, this one laid out each partner's obligation toward the other. It carefully tallied the value and content of the dowry the bride would bring to the marriage. It noted that the groom swore to provide a safe home and to protect his wife. It also stated that the groom promised to have sex with his bride. Naturally, things have changed since 499 B.C. Particularly in more secular, Western countries, romantic love now tops most people's list of reasons for getting married, not dowries or personal safety, and many would balk at the idea of negotiating their impending marriage like a business arrangement. But maybe they shouldn't. Whatever life brought, Tamut and Ananiah knew without a doubt what each expected from their marriage and from each other, and their short life spans probably made their contract relatively easy to fulfill.

Modern couples have it a little tougher. While many think they know what their spouse expects from the marriage, they're often wrong because they didn't negotiate beforehand. In addition, they don't renegotiate as they navigate the challenges and transitions that every marriage endures. Yet those couples who can adjust the expectations they had on their wedding day—who believe their marriage contracts are malleable, not fixed—are in a much better position to enjoy a lifetime of happiness and fulfillment together.

The Implicit Marriage Contract

While you may not have sat down like Tamut and Ananiah and hammered out a formal, explicit agreement that outlined your expectations of marriage, when you wed, regardless of the type of ceremony you chose or the vows you spoke, you entered into an implicit contract with your spouse: "I will always love you the way I do now." You also entered into many other agreements, "terms and conditions" that reinforce and help implement your marriage contract, covering everything from who will do what around the house to expectations about fidelity, religion, and whether to have children.

You may have established some of these agreements after having explicit conversations with your spouse, but others you may have simply taken for granted because that's the way things have always been: "He brings me flowers every Friday, so he'll always bring me flowers on Fridays." "She loves to cook elaborate meals. Our kids will have such sophisticated palates!" It rarely occurs to us, in the heady days of early love, that the implicit agreements we enter into with our spouses could change, that one day your husband might take a look at the bank account and decide that spending thirty-five dollars on a bouquet every Friday is an easily abandoned expense, or that your wife might lose her enthusiasm for cooking once your third child is born. Unfortunately, it is almost inevitable that one or both marriage partners will eventually break at least some of the implicit promises they made on their wedding day.

The reason for this is not that human beings are inherently untrustworthy or incapable of commitment. The reason is simply that over time, people change, sometimes by choice, sometimes due to circumstance and the demands of life. I've often heard people sigh regretfully, "She used to be so carefree. Where did that girl go?" or, "He's not the man I married ten years ago." That's right, he's not. And that girl you married? She's got two kids and a small business to manage now. It is unreasonable to expect the people we wed to stay exactly the same over time, and therefore it's also unreasonable to expect that our feelings for each other will always remain identical.

In addition, sometimes we inadvertently breach our marriage's implicit contracts because we neglect to tell our partner about pacts we made with ourselves. For example, it might not occur to a woman to inform her husband specifically that her family will not be complete until she has three children. Surely he knows—she's daydreamed about her future with him many times. What she doesn't realize is that his ideal family looks like the one in which he grew up, with only two children. Everything is fine until they have two kids and she starts talking about planning for the third, only to discover that he has no interest. Suddenly they are faced with an enormous stumbling block.

Renegotiate Your Marriage is meant to help you over that stumbling block—and each one that comes after. *All* marriages eventually hit not just one, but many. At some point, every married person will take an incredulous look at his or her spouse and think, "I can't believe I married this person. What was I thinking?" But when this happens, you don't have to keep your fingers crossed that you'll feel differently in a few months. You can take active steps to recalibrate your feelings and remember the love that drew you to your spouse in the first place. You can diffuse any anger or disappointment you may feel and find understanding and compassion instead. You can inspire your partner to work with you to rebuild the trust and desire you once shared. You can navigate your way around almost any impasse in your marriage—if you are willing to renegotiate with your spouse, and with yourself.

Redefining Renegotiation

Traditionally, most people think of negotiation as a process of give and take: "I'll give you X so that I can get Y." When successfully renegotiating a marriage, though, couples need to think of the process as give and give. "I'll give you X—more sex, more attention, more time to yourself, more back rubs, more whatever you ask for. No strings attached. I will do it because I know you need it, and because it will make you understand how much I love you. I will do it even when I don't feel like it, because I know it matters to you. And eventually, I'll get most of what I need back in spades."

This recommendation may seem counterintuitive, especially if you feel that your essential needs are not being met, or you're worn out and wounded. Why should you have to make the first move? Well, someone does, and though it may not seem fair that it should be you when you've already done so much, if you're reading this book, it's because you still believe your marriage can be saved or improved. Giving, even when you don't feel like it, is a crucial first step to getting your marriage on firmer footing. A renegotiation can only take place when your spouse feels safe. If you can create a calm environment and an atmosphere of generosity, your partner will have a much easier time imagining a happy, secure future with you. As you'll see in many of the real-life examples in this book, generosity begets generosity; loving actions beget loving actions. The positive feelings your efforts will evoke in your partner will help smooth the way toward a mutually acceptable renegotiation, one in which you get back as much as you give. Try it. At this point, you have little to lose and everything to gain.

The Benefits of Negotiating a Long-Term, Happy Marriage

The difference between marriages that last and those that don't is that the couple in the former believe that the implicit marriage contract is flexible and open to renegotiation, and the couple in the latter believe it is set in stone. Partners who can successfully renegotiate the transitions that every relationship experiences also have another thing in common: they strongly believe in the value and benefits of a lifetime commitment. A person who is committed to staying in a marriage for the long haul is far more open to negotiation than someone who sees divorce as an option. Negotiation is for the tenacious.

We live in a society where the idea of staying together "for better and for worse" seems almost absurd. Why should anyone put up with the hassle of "worse" when they know they could get "better" if they just cut their losses and moved on to different relationships that reflect their current needs, dreams, and desires?

The answer is that it's good for us. Studies have shown that people in long-term marriages are happier, healthier, and more contented than those who have a series of broken relationships. In addition, when compared to people who cohabitate, married people:

- Live longer
- Have less psychological illness
- Exhibit fewer risky behaviors and suffer fewer economic hardships
- Have more sex

Given the legalization of same-sex marriage in several states at the time of this book's publication, it's worth noting that these advantages are not reserved for heterosexual partnerships; the benefits of marriage transcend gender orientation.

A mature, committed, long-term relationship offers you the greatest chance to fulfill your utmost emotional, physical, and psychological potential. The longer someone knows you and the more experiences you share, the more opportunities your partner has to offer valuable, useful, and reliable feedback and advice. In addition, long-term relationships provide a sense of safety, which affords more comfort taking risks, expanding your horizons, and receiving constructive criticism.

Having a lifelong partner is a scary but thrilling concept. It means building a series of shared memories that define you, both as a person and as a couple. It means allowing your spouse to tell you things about yourself that may be difficult to hear, but will improve who you are as a human being. Who else will have the nerve to tell you when you are unintentionally insulting Uncle Fred, or once again being too passive with your father, or overspending money you may not have, or gaining too much weight, or getting too thin? Your spouse knows you better than anyone, and that's priceless. By following the strategies and information presented in *Renegotiate Your Marriage*, you will not only be able to create a stronger, happier marriage, but a deeper understanding of yourself.

Become a Master Negotiator

Renegotiate Your Marriage will allow you to recapture (or reinvent) the relationship you most desired when you said, "I do." It will teach you everything you need to know to identify when and how to make the necessary revisions or adjustments to your marriage bond and keep your relationship strong. It will also offer tips on how to negotiate your marriage contract early on so that it's flexible yet strong enough to withstand whatever life throws at it. Some renegotiations take just a few well-orchestrated dialogues; many take weeks and even months of subtle gestures, gentle words, and thoughtful planning. By studying how other couples have navigated the various phases of marriage, from the birth of a child to a job loss, from illness to a spiritual awakening, and even plain old boredom, you will learn:

- How to identify when your needs have changed
- How to express them in an unthreatening way
- How to accept your spouse's needs
- How to rekindle desire and enhance your sensual life
- How to mediate the differences between you and your partner that could threaten your relationship
- How to put your partner ahead of your principles
- How to increase your ability to support, encourage, and empathize with each other

You'll find that there are repeated patterns and similar elements to many successful negotiations, but endless ways to adapt them creatively for your particular situation.

No matter how broken your marriage seems, you can renegotiate new life into it. It may not sound romantic to think of your twosome as a deal that needs to be re-examined from time to time, turned over and inspected for quality, but renegotiating your marriage contract on a regular basis is the single best thing you can do to fortify the foundation of a long-term, happy union. Indeed, your newfound negotiating skills can help you achieve a whole fresh level of communication with your spouse.

Every Marriage Needs to Be Renegotiated

Renegotiate Your Marriage is for every couple, whether you're newlyweds, raising children, or contemplating your silver anniversary. In the forty years that I've been practicing couples therapy, there is one thing that has proven itself to be true again and again: most of the marriages that last experience the same things as the marriages that don't. Most people have in-laws that drive them crazy. Lots of couples feel overwhelmed by the responsibility of child rearing. Many families will face periods of financial instability or poor health. Couples have sexual dry spells. These changes do not have to break a marriage. In fact, sustaining a healthy, happy marriage has little to do with what we experience as a couple.

Renegotiating a relationship involves hard work, but anything worthwhile does. And while the road can be rocky at times, it can also be exhilarating and a lot of fun. It is worth the effort because a healthy, long-term marriage is one of the most enlightening experiences one can have. I hope this book will help you and your partner enjoy this bequest so it can provide a lifetime of fulfillment for both of you.

Part 1

Renegotiating How to Love One Another

Love is a choice, but sex and desire are biology. Everything we do when we court, flirt, mate, and commit is fueled by a complicated interaction of emotions and hormones. If you want to increase the level of intimacy and love in your relationship, it's in your best interest to be aware of what emotions fuel which hormones, and practice the behaviors that will get them flowing as much as possible. The more in tune you are with your sensuality, sexuality, your needs, moods, and cravings, the more capable you are of being sensitive to your partner's as well, and of reciprocating in kind.

Chapter 1

Sex: Positioning Yourself for a Better Marriage

There is no fulfilling love relationship without a satisfying sensual life, yet sex is often one of the most contentious issues in a marriage. After a few years, a few children, a few strained backs, the couple that couldn't keep their hands off each other can become the couple that doesn't even kiss each other good night. It is biologically impossible to sustain the original levels of profound emotions that initially spark a romance—ardor, passion, excitement, affirmation—and form the foundation of the couple's unspoken bond. But if you renegotiate your expectations you can rekindle and then tend those fires so that they never go out. Best of all, it will only take about a week to see results in the form of improved intimacy and communication.

Jeffrey and Elisha

Jeffrey bolted up around 3 A.M., startled by the screaming siren of a fire engine zooming past his city street. He looked over and saw his wife, Elisha, sleeping peacefully next to him. *God, I have a beautiful wife*, he thought. He didn't wake her, though. Years ago he wouldn't have hesitated, but tonight he winced as he remembered what had happened the last time he had tried to make love to her in the middle of the night. She'd snarled at him for pawing her while she was asleep. When he'd said, "Remember our honeymoon? We didn't sleep through a single full night," she had snapped, "We didn't have three kids back then. I took care of everyone all day, I'm tired, and right now I think I'd trade a lifetime of celibacy for a good night's rest."

Jeffrey's feelings of desire had quickly morphed into anger and coldness.

Now as Jeffrey watched his wife sleep, he couldn't even remember the last time they'd made love. How had they allowed so much distance to come between them in just a few short years?

A Common Problem

If Jeffrey and Elisha's situation sounds familiar to you, you're not alone. Countless couples have experienced similar sexual strain. By the time they seek help, some of them haven't had sex in a decade or more. Many times they arrive at my office prepared to air their gripes, assuming that if they solve their problems first, their sex lives will get better. It can come as quite a shock when their first homework assignment is to get physical. The positive effects of skin-to-skin contact on a relationship are very much a chicken-or-the-egg phenomenon. Sex inspires feelings of comfort and a desire to communicate. But the same is true in reverse. The more we touch, the safer we feel; the safer we feel, the more we open up; the more we open up, the greater possibility for sex. And that's a goal I have for almost every couple I meet—as much sex as possible. As important as verbal communication is to a relationship, creating renewed sensuality is often a crucial first step to successful renegotiations.

The First Contract

Physical intimacy is the glue that holds a marriage together. It is one of the primary unspoken pacts a couple makes in the early days of their relationship. Will we have it? Will we like it? Will we want more? Will we want to have it with anyone else? If a couple can't agree on those basic answers, the relationship will have a hard time moving forward. The sexual contract affects every phase of marriage, of which there are three: the lust phase, the romantic phase, and the attachment phase.

New couples are physiologically designed to lust for each other. The strong desire they feel provides a chemical high of testosterone and adrenalin, in both men and women, loosens inhibitions, and fuels a desire to procreate. Without lust, there would be little motivation for people to come together and form relationships; our selfish instincts simply wouldn't allow it. The lust phase is a magical time that lays the foundation for memories that couples can use as a touchstone later on, like when you're eighty-five and turn to each other, smiling, and say, "Hey, remember that time in the swimming pool in Mexico?" During the early stages of a relationship, it's almost impossible for many couples to imagine that they will not always lust for each other. An implicit promise is forged: "I will always want you the way I want you right now."

If a couple is lucky, lust turns into love, and they progress to the romantic stage, in which partners court. This is generally when the idea of marriage occurs. Finally, after about two years, they reach the attachment phase, as described by Helen Fisher in her book, *Why We Love*. That stage is where couples must contend with a dramatic change, often one of the first significant challenges to their happiness.

Understanding Attachment —————————————————————————

There are three forms of attachment: secure, anxious, and insecure. The first people we connect to are our parents, and the quality of our attachment to them is often replicated in how we relate to our mates. *Secure* attachments are formed when our parents respond appropriately to our needs and make us feel safe and surrounded by love. Overprotective parents can often cause *anxious* attachments by undermining their children's confidence and convincing them that the world is a dangerous place. *Insecure* attachments are formed when a parent is negligent or distant, and doesn't provide enough nurturing care, emotional support, and guidance. No one parents perfectly, of course, but how secure, anxious, or insecure grownups become is directly related to the overall feeling of security, anxiety, or distance they had in their homes growing up.

If you had a difficult relationship with a parent, or if you know your spouse grew up in a complicated home life, keep that in mind when you reach this phase in your relationship. As your original implicit contracts are tested, one or both of you may need special attention to achieve a sense of security.

The attachment phase of a romantic relationship can be a delight, yielding feelings of calm, peace, and security that facilitate child rearing. It can also be accompanied by a shift in the amount of time you spend having sex. With time, our interests and habits change, which alters our original, compelling sexual desire. Stress increases, careers ramp up, free time and energy are sapped. If there are children, they clamor for attention. It's easy to move sex further down our list of priorities. The hot relationship we once enjoyed becomes a distant memory until suddenly we wonder where the magic went.

If this sounds familiar, the worst thing you can do is accept it. While it's okay to allow a change in your relationship's sexual customs—whereas once you always went to bed at the same time, now your wife stays up to catch up on her social networking sites;

the hour you used to spend holding each other and talking after making love fell victim long ago to a desperate need to get as much sleep as possible before the damned alarm goes off again—it's not okay to forgo sex. Sex is the royal road to emotional intimacy, a bond that satisfies the body, heart, mind, and spirit.

When you have sex with your spouse, it's like having a deep conversation. In essence, you're sharing information about each other in a private language no one knows but you. If you fall out of step with each other sexually, you block the door to communication and create obstacles for renegotiation. That's why I send people to bed even when they say they can barely stand each other.

Lack of Sexual Impulse and Desire ——————————

Even if you still hold hands and cuddle, if you're not having intercourse, no matter how old you are, there is something unresolved that is influencing your lack of sexual impulse and desire. Take note of how often you have sex with your partner. If it is once a month, force yourself to lead the charge for reengagement and ramp it up. It is a slippery slope— the less you do it, the less you feel like doing it; the more you do it, the more you want it. Do not wait until your sensual life is lying comatose to take action.

Nathan and Helena

When Nathan and Helena came for counseling, Helena was angry because after seven years of marriage, she was tired of feeling like her affection toward Nathan was being met with derision. Predictably, the angrier she became, the less she wanted to have sex. Nathan complained, but Helena, stung by his perceived indifference, preferred to ignore him. The strongest thing holding them together was their son.

When I asked them to tell me about themselves and what they perceived to be the problem, they couldn't even make it ten minutes without bickering about the details. Finally, I told them I didn't want to know anymore. What I did want was for them to have sex every day for a week. They both looked at me like I was nuts. That was fine with me; at least I had them agreeing on something. Nathan and Helena seemed doubtful, but eventually agreed to give it a try.

When Nathan and Helena returned a week later, I noticed a marked change. While they were no means touchy-feely, Helena's words and gestures were noticeably softer. Nathan had a more relaxed posture and had stopped crossing his arms whenever his wife spoke. I asked how the lovemaking sessions were going. They looked at each other tentatively, and smiled. "It's a pain to manage, but it's better than fighting all of the time," Helena said. Nathan laughed and agreed. I advised they should continue to have scheduled sex at least four times a week for the next month.

Negotiation 101

Under your new contract, you can no longer resist your spouse's advances the way you did before. You don't always have to say yes, but no more rolling your eyes or pulling away. Rather, if your spouse starts to make a move and you really don't want to engage, smile kindly and say, "Honey, I love you but I am just beat tonight. Let me get a good night's sleep, and tomorrow I'll give you a rain check." And then stick to that promise. Do not become a liar, because then you are sabotaging the safe environment you are trying to create for one another. If the next day comes and you're still not in the mood, do whatever it takes to get there (see the sidebar "Get in the Mood Any Way You Can").

Opening the Door to Renegotiation

Sex is the fastest way to produce oxytocin, otherwise known as the love hormone. Several studies have shown that oxytocin eases stress, promotes attachment, and improves social skills. Ironically, if you're in a stalemate, the best way to end it is by having sex. It gives you closeness beyond words. It is much easier to discuss painful or delicate subjects calmly, rationally, and lovingly when you have tapped into the tenderness that sex elicits. It protects a couple from other pressures. It is easier to weather in-laws and crying babies and money troubles and the realities of everyday life when your body is filled with lots of sex hormones.

If the idea of reaching for your spouse seems terrifying or even distasteful, force yourself to do it anyway. That is, do it if you truly want your relationship to last a lifetime. Although Helena and Nathan didn't relish the idea of making love at first, their commitment to building a lifelong relationship helped them work through their initial resistance. Their increased intimacy compelled them to let down their defenses and find the courage to start talking about what was bothering them, which in turn allowed them to start renegotiating how they could each best express and accept affection.

Over time, Helena felt safe enough to expose her vulnerability, and told Nathan how his inability to accept her affection or appreciate her efforts was hurting her. Without taking an accusatory tone, she reminded him of how he had barely looked at the scrapbook she had lovingly made for their anniversary, and how she had felt when he'd scoffed, "Seriously? Gosh, we must be getting old," after she surprised him with a weekend to a Bermuda resort. Nathan admitted that sentimental gestures made him uncomfortable and that he'd learned to dismiss them because his mother had always made him feel weak for wanting extra attention or encouragement. He promised to practice being more receptive to his wife's affection. In return, Helena promised to stay calm while telling her husband when he hurt her.

Unlike other members of the animal kingdom, we can control our impulses and desires. We can decide for ourselves whether to be open to our emotions or build a wall around them. Helena and Nathan put aside their pride and hurt feelings for the sake of something bigger: their marriage. Within a year, they had a second baby. As soon as Helena was ready to have sex again after the birth, they resumed regular lovemaking sessions, averaging three times per week. They kept that average steady through the blow-up fight they had over whether Helena's mother could move in for a month, and through the months when Nathan was pulling all-nighters at the office to hit his deadline. Regardless of how they felt or what was going on around them, they didn't let the frequency of their lovemaking decline.

Forging a New Sexual Contract: How to Start Having Sex Again

1. Pick the right time.

Just because you've decided it's time to renegotiate your sexual contract doesn't mean, of course, that your partner will immediately be on board. Getting to yes may take much foreplay—head rubs, foot rubs, back rubs, cuddling, and persistence. Persistence with kindness pays off. Negotiate a minimum number of times to have sex per month.

Also, be open to changing when you normally have it. Just because you are used to getting busy right before bed and on the weekends doesn't mean it should always be that way. Experiment with making love when you wake up, at the beginning of the week, before stress and exhaustion take their toll on you.

Learning about the positive correlation between longevity and an active sex life may also help convince your partner to renegotiate. For a list of helpful titles, see the Appendix at the back of this book.

2. Pick the right place . . . any place.

Changing the venue of your lovemaking sessions can be titillating. If boredom has set in your marital bed, head for the kitchen, bathtub, couch, living room floor, vacation resort, sleazy hotel . . . it doesn't matter where you make love, just venture off the beaten path. The excitement will draw you closer.

3. Pick the right person.

The idea is not just to have more sex, but to have sex with your partner. Getting those hormones from someone else won't do a thing to increase intimacy with your spouse. It'll likely just make you feel even more distant. If you're feeling tempted to look elsewhere, turning your sexual contract on its head might do the trick to bringing excitement back into your bedroom. Try altering roles, so that the person who traditionally initiates takes a more passive role, while the partner who is usually more receptive assumes the lead. Become a new partner for your lover and eliminate any risk he or she will look elsewhere. Visit your local sex toy shop, buy sensual creams, and look for seductive lingerie or cute boxer shorts. Women love to see their men in something other than plain tighty-whities.

4. Pick the right positions.

There are myriad ways of making love, but over time, couples frequently do the same thing night after night. Experiment with new positions, sex toys, and techniques. If oral sex has fallen by the wayside, integrate it back into your repertoire. Acting out fantasies can be stimulating, too. In the event you're stuck for ideas, pick up a copy of the *Kama Sutra*. It has been a sexual resource for thousands of years, with good reason.

5. Pick the right reasons.

Lots of couples make the mistake of making love only when they are in the mood, yet it's a fantastic way to smooth troubled waters. So make love after a fight. Make love to gear up for a date. Make love to celebrate the fact that it's Friday. Make up any reason you can to make love.

Changing Your Definition of Sex

The definition of sex can change over time. Illness, impotency, and injuries can force couples to alter the way they define it. If you're not able to have traditional intercourse, expand your definition. Mutual masturbation, oral sex, erotic massage—the point is to touch each other in a way that is exclusive to your partner. This will give your marriage the physical intimacy most couples need to feel valued, supported, and privileged.

Negotiating When Met with Resistance

Renegotiating a sexual contract—from one in which sex is a treat bestowed when things are going well, to one in which sex is a primary channel for regular communication in good times and bad—can save a marriage and launch further renegotiations to problem aspects of a relationship. But what do you do if you decide you want to renegotiate your sex life and you meet with resistance?

Jeffrey's Opening Move

Jeffrey took a few days to recover from his memory of Elisha's most recent rejection, keeping his distance both physically and emotionally. But he knew something had to change. His parents had started sleeping in separate bedrooms around his eighth birthday, and he had suffered growing up in a cold, emotionally barren home. Jeffrey had sworn he would never be in a marriage like theirs. He was not going to fail his kids the way he felt his parents had failed him.

One night he got into bed while Elisha was reading her paperback and started nuzzling her neck. She made a face and swatted him away.

"Not now."

"Please?"

"I don't feel like it!"

"Okay. When will you feel like it?"

"I don't know."

"How about tomorrow?"

"I'm tired!"

"Honey, I know you're tired, but you might be tired until the baby goes to college. Please put the book down and look at me. We haven't had sex in months. I miss you. I think we've gotten ourselves into some kind of cycle that is only going to get worse if we don't do something now to fix it. We used to love having sex together. Maybe with a little effort we could find a way to get some of our mojo back. I want the kids to grow up seeing their parents be physically affectionate with each other."

Jeffrey approached Elisha gently, in a nonthreatening way, and his plea got Elisha's attention. She found herself annoyed with him a lot of the time, but she still loved him, and now she was moved by his honesty and his determination to be a better husband and parent than his own father had been. She knew his parents and didn't want to wind up like them, either. She intuited that this would be a bad time to reject his advances. Problem was, she really was tired, and she wasn't sure she would be any more in the mood tomorrow, or the next day, or the day after that. Surely he didn't want her to just go through the motions?

Just Do It

In a recent study published in the *Journal of Sex & Marital Therapy*, researchers found that 54 percent of men and 42 percent of women polled were unhappy with the frequency of sex in their lives. The majority wanted to have more sex, suggesting that other obligations were getting in the way of their physical relations. According to Anthony Smith, the coauthor of the study, "If people value sex as an important part of their relationship . . . they need to put sex higher up the priority list."

So, actually going through the motions is exactly what you need to do if you want to strengthen your relationship. There's a three-thousand-year-old biblical teaching, supported by scientific research that essentially dictates, "Do it first, and feel it afterward." For example, if you act lovingly toward someone, you will start to feel love. If you have sex, you'll want to have more sex. Eventually, you'll develop a taste for sex and the brain chemicals testosterone, adrenalin, and dopamine, among others, will take over, making you want more sex like you did in the early days of your relationship. Often, we convince ourselves we are no longer sexual beings after long dry spells.

The truth is, we are all sexual beings. Like most feel-good activities, sex is habit-forming. The more you have, the more you will want, and the more you will want to be near the person who can make you feel that good.

Get in the Mood Any Way You Can

If you're serious about strengthening your sexual connection to your spouse, you've got to get in the mood. But many of the things that keep you from feeling particularly sexy still exist. The kids are still around, work still beckons whether you're home or at the office, and there are still a million household chores to do, bills to pay, and e-mails to return. Don't let any of that stop you. Tell the kids that mom is taking a bath tonight. Stop by the store and pick up something special to share with your wife after the children are in bed. Lock the bathroom door for five minutes and masturbate. Do whatever you need to get yourself in the mood. If you do this often enough—if you get in touch with your sexual side and remember what it feels like to want it—you may not have to do any prep work the next time your spouse whispers in your ear, "How about tonight?" But if you do, that's okay. Prep work is fun, too!

Jeffrey and Elisha Renegotiate More

Elisha made love to her husband that night, and the next night when he initiated again. When he started pressing at her nightclothes again two days later, she felt the old irritation flare up.

Then she took a breath, and instead of pushing him away, which she knew would hurt his feelings, she took his hands in hers and said, "I know we need to have more sex, and I've enjoyed the last few times we've made love, but I don't think I'm going to be able to keep up with you at this rate. How much sex do you think you'll need to feel like we're getting emotionally closer? What is it exactly that you want to see happen?"

Jeffrey's opening move got the negotiation process started, and then Elisha made sure the couple achieved their goal by insisting that they specifically hammer out what their new sexual contract was going to look like. When you're doing this, it's good to keep the following points in mind:

1. Recognize you both have more power than you realize.

It is always easier to say no or to withdraw than to take a risk and open yourself up to rejection. But ultimately opening yourself up is the most personally empowering skill you can develop. It will serve you well in every aspect of your life.

2. The middle is a good place to be.

Normally, one partner is going to want more sex than the other. You can't change your partner's biology, but you can change your own. Just as you need to "use it or lose it," you can also use it to regain it. In the beginning of your negotiation strike a happy medium when deciding the frequency of lovemaking. If you have a stronger libido than your partner, she might be more open to accepting your overtures if you shower her with more compliments outside of the bedroom. If you are the one less interested, you might substitute more sex with an offer for extra loving gestures throughout the day, such as providing a foot massage, giving your husband a half hour of privacy when he comes home from work, or doing a dreaded chore without being asked. Never bestow with an expectation of a return, especially sex. Ironically, though, the rewards will come. Kind actions like these almost always lay the groundwork for warmer interactions.

3. The details are unimportant.

Your spouse likes sex first thing in the morning; you prefer it at night. You like to keep the lights on, she wants them off. Stop arguing about petty details and get busy. You're far more likely to get what you prefer once the ball is in motion again.

If You're Having Sex, Might As Well Make It Great!

Since you've renegotiated a new contract that says you're going to have more sex, you might as well negotiate for the best you've ever had. That means you're going to have to talk about it, probably more than you're accustomed to.

Discussing sensuality can be difficult. You need to be honest but diplomatic. Nobody likes to be told what he or she is doing in bed is anything less than fabulous. However, there are ways to ensure the conversation goes as smoothly as possible. Start by saying what you like that the other person already does and then suggest an add-on. "I love the way you touch my legs, could you move your hands slightly upward next time? That would feel even yummier."

1. Choose your time wisely.

Don't engage in negotiations while you're in the act. People are at their most vulnerable when they're making love, and won't take kindly to changing the game while in the throes of passion. Similarly, broaching the subject when your spouse just gets in the door after a long day of work is dicey. Ideally, talk when you're both relaxed and the kids are in bed, or you're enjoying an outdoor activity.

2. Avoid the blame game.

Opening a sexual negotiation with accusatory phrases like, "Why do you always _____?" or "Do you really need to _____?" is a recipe for disaster. Remember, you are trying to parlay a better sex life together, not score points. Take ownership of your recommendations with phrases like, "I think I could do better to help us have more fun in bed, but I'm a little nervous. When I approach you, it would help me to keep up my courage if you could let me cuddle you, kiss you, touch your breasts, nibble your ear, stroke your penis, etc." That way, you can both progress without attacking or shaming the other.

3. Be respectful.

Remember, your spouse's feelings are just as valid as yours. You may not always agree or understand them, but the important thing is to try to build a bridge between you.

4. Honesty is the best policy.

If you don't like baby talk or kissing with too much tongue, be honest. Offer suggestions you enjoy. Remember, your partner isn't a mind reader, and neither are you. When you're unsure what your spouse would like, ask in an inviting way that demonstrates compassion. For example, "I want to please you sexually. What makes you happy? Rubbing your feet, scratching your back, my telling you a sexual fantasy? I'd love to know!"

5. Listen.

Intimate listening increases feelings of safety and even fulfillment. Best of all, if you listen intently to your husband or wife, you increase the chances the favor will be returned. When your partner is unclear or lost for words, ask questions. Meet everything he or she says with acceptance. Tender gestures like laying your hand upon your spouse's knee or touching her shoulder can melt barriers.

Instead of reacting, stay calm and let your partner talk. If the conversation becomes accusatory or angry, remain quiet until he finishes speaking. Consider that most people get defensive when they feel vulnerable. By maintaining a calm, receptive attitude, you'll be able to renegotiate your contract in a way that satisfies you both. Remember, negotiation takes practice. If your initial conversation is stressful or strained, give yourself credit for taking the first step and schedule another talk when you're both relaxed and receptive. Eventually, your persistence will pay off.

A great marriage requires sensuality. It adds vibrancy and Technicolor to our ordinary existence. When a couple renegotiates their old sexual contract, they're automatically paving the way for a happier, healthier, longer, and far more fulfilled life together.

Chapter 2

Desire: Stoking the Fire and Keeping It Burning

If sex is the glue that keeps a marriage together, desire is the fuel that keeps it moving forward. Without it marriages can die, so it's imperative to do whatever you can to maintain that flame's life. Contrary to what most people think, however, desire has little to do with sex. Rekindling longing will not be accomplished by coming up with sexual lures or a shopping spree at Victoria's Secret (though that could help you carry on the great sex life you'll negotiate if you commit to the wisdom in Chapter 1). Rather, the most effective strategy for eliciting want in your spouse is to concern yourself less with getting him or her to fall in love with you again, and more with falling in love with yourself.

All Fired Up

New couples work hard to make themselves as interesting and attractive as possible to each other during the early stage of a relationship. Every detail is a revelation, an opportunity to find more common ground. "You play ice hockey? I love ice hockey!" "You hate cauliflower? My cauliflower gratin will change your mind."

"I've never been to Spain but I've always wanted to go. Tell me more about your time there." Your new love thinks your anecdote about the frog in the log cabin—the one that elicits a "here we go again" roll of the eyes from your friends every time you tell it—is fresh and hilarious.

The more each person brings to the table, the more time spent discussing mutual interests and exploring each other's thoughts and ideas, the more pleasing the relationship. Though the anticipation of sex is still a huge draw, you also start to yearn for the refreshing take on life that the other person demonstrates. You still experience lust, but now you also sense desire. As your feelings deepen, it begins to seem as if no one else could be capable of making you feel as good and happy as the person you're with right now, and you want to be together as much as possible. And so couples become monogamous, and often marry. An unspoken contract of desire is formed: "I want you and you want me; we find each other interesting and attractive and it will always remain that way."

The Rut of Routine

But newness fades, and when it does it can be hard to live up to the terms of that implied agreement. The very things that once provided a sexy spark between you might bore you. Maybe you lose interest in cooking and stop making lavish meals. Maybe your spouse's fascination with motorcycles means he spends increasing amounts of time away from home on the road. While once you obsessed over what you'd wear on a date and meticulously planned every detail of the itinerary, now your dates, which might be few and far between, rarely venture far from the casual dinner-and-a-movie-formula. The love between the two of you might still be there, but the desire, that yearning you once felt when the other wasn't around—that faded a long time ago.

Step 1: Become the "Someone New"

Change, novelty, and emotional growth trigger dopamine, one of the main "love chemicals" that originally drew you and your spouse together. In the attachment phase of a relationship, dopamine manifests itself through a sense of desire. Without dopamine, it's hard to maintain the active connection that successful marriages depend upon. When desire fades, boredom increases. People start to think that the solution to their boredom is to find someone new. But you can be that someone new to your spouse and renew your implicit contract of desire if you can get those levels of dopamine raging again. How? By making yourself as desirable as possible.

Find Your Passion

Rekindling desire is an entirely selfish pursuit. Paradoxically, the best way to elicit want in someone else is not to devote yourself to the object of your affection, but to devote yourself to yourself. You have to make yourself as dopamine-inducing as possible; that is, new, exciting, surprising, and stimulating. Think about it, is there anyone more appealing than a person who is bursting with enthusiasm, who is excited to talk about new experiences, and who welcomes you to share in them? Not really, right? It's up to you to become that appealing person. "Hold on," you might be thinking. "Shouldn't my spouse love me for who I am? Why do I have to start jumping through hoops to earn back his or her affection?"

The goal is not to become someone you're not. Rather, the goal is to become your best self. This is something we could all be striving to do every day, but most of us get caught up in the frenzy of life and let opportunities for personal growth fall by the wayside. Routine and stagnation is murder on a marriage, but when each spouse cultivates his or her interests and remains engaged in the world, dopamine levels remain steady, boredom is kept at bay, and marriage stays fresh. Finding your passion and indulging in it may feel selfish, but in fact it's one of the most loving gifts you can offer your spouse.

Rekindling Desire Begins with Self-Evaluation

When you're trying to figure out what interest to pursue, make sure that it's something that expands your horizons. Don't cling to the activities that helped define you in the early days of your courtship. Push yourself, learn, and experiment. You may be passionate about your child, but you're not going to see fresh desire flare up in your wife's eyes by centering even more of your conversation on child rearing. Getting involved in, for example, grassroots efforts to reform public education, though, would probably be a challenge and take you down paths you haven't traveled before. The new interest or activity you pursue must be something that forces you to stretch your emotional or intellectual muscles, maybe even lead you out of your comfort zone. It should bring you into a new social circle, take you to novel places, and teach you something you didn't know before.

This is not the time to stick with the safe and familiar. This is the moment to do the things you've always talked about doing but found an excuse not to pursue. No more excuses.

Take Charge

Don't wait for your spouse's permission to start expanding your horizons. Though usually it's a good idea to talk to your partner when you're about to make big decisions or changes in your life, this is one time where it's okay to decide what you want to do without checking in first. Part of becoming more desirable is to inject a little something unexpected into your relationship, and reveal yourself in a different light than the one your spouse has seen you in for the past however-many years. The change will do you both good.

As the time you start to invest in your new pursuit begins to pay off—you start to win chess tournaments, you earn a new color belt in tae kwon do, you hold your own in a conversation about politics, in Japanese—your enthusiasm will grow, and quite likely start to infect your partner. It may take time, but you should soon see your partner showing interest in what you're doing, much like he or she did back when you were first getting to know each other. Now you have negotiated a change in your partner's desire through your influence. At the least, she has taken new notice of you, and at best she might see you are flourishing and decide to join you as you learn to kayak or surf. Either way, you've introduced added excitement into your home.

Tips for Achieving Desire Through Self-Fulfillment

1. Negotiate with yourself to get over your fears of change or to kick-start your motivation. Ask yourself the following question: "If I were brave enough, I would try _____." Write five things you'd like to try.
2. Choose one of the things on your list. It can be a hobby like making homemade pasta, a competitive endeavor like running a marathon, or a long-term goal like getting a graduate degree. Select the activity that fills your heart with excitement.
3. Make a list of three tiny steps you can take toward your goal. Set a deadline by which to meet each of these goals. Be firm but gentle with your deadlines. Self-expansion should not involve shame or blame. All it involves is being open to altering your original contract with yourself as to who you were, are now, and who you will become.
4. Love the person you are becoming. Be proud of yourself.
5. After you've made three steps toward your goal, tell your spouse about your plan. Do not expect immediate celebration. Your spouse will likely go through a transition period before becoming comfortable with your change. Give your partner the time he needs to get used to the new contract you are asking him to accept.

When we renegotiate, by default we are asking each other to accept change. Accepting change necessitates going through three phases: an end, a readjustment, and a new beginning. We will explore these phases more in Chapter 5.

Continue Despite Resistance

Continue to pursue your goal, regardless of your spouse's response. Ideally, your other half will immediately support your new interest, and even get involved. In this fantasy, the minute you enter a race, she will create a hand-painted sign to wave from the sidelines as you run past. Or when you mention that you learned to make an amazing white gazpacho in your cooking class, he will suggest inviting a few friends over and serving it. It's even possible to imagine that your spouse will ask if he or she can join you in your new activity. Suddenly, you've got built-in opportunities to bond and remember how much you enjoy spending time together. Notice if romance starts to perk up. Pay close attention, you may inspire your other half to resurrect or discover some new dreams of her own. When you do, reinforce it with bravos, sex, hugs, and support.

Most change, however, does meet with resistance. It's part of the transition stage. If your spouse does not respond with the enthusiasm you'd hoped for, don't let that discourage you. Create persistence as your most important asset. Continue to try to share your new experiences. Make it clear you want to be inclusive, but resist shoving anything down his throat, and/or punishing him by locking him out of your new world. Reaching a middle ground gives you the best chance of seeing your new contract received favorably. Give your partner empathy for his discomfort. He didn't ask for this ending, but with your encouragement and patience eventually he will enter the new beginning with you.

Step 2: Show Your Need

Unfortunately, a partner can sometimes feel left behind when you move into a world that he might not have even known you were interested in joining. You can prevent your other half from feeling abandoned or threatened by making sure to make it clear that you still need him.

Showing that we need someone isn't always easy. Highly intelligent, competent people, in particular, often have a hard time with it. They mistake showing need with being needy, though the two are very different. Neediness opens up an insatiable void that your partner will fruitlessly try to fill, which will leave him feeling depleted and inept. Your need, though, makes your partner feel important. It's the secret weapon in building the desire that brings a couple closer. It isn't accomplished by demanding that your spouse come home earlier so you can get to your class without rushing. You could conceivably hire a babysitter or ask a friend or family member to do that. Show your spouse that you need him by asking something of him that no one else can provide. If you were a runner, you might say, "It would mean so much to me if you would come to my race so I can hear you cheer for me when I go by," or, "My Japanese is getting good enough that I think I'm ready to use it. Let's start saving for a trip to Japan together!" You create a strong negotiation move by making it clear that although you're enjoying your newfound passion, part of the enjoyment is in sharing what you've learned, both about the activity and about yourself, with your partner.

Renegotiate Your Needs

Maybe you're not sure what you need from your spouse. Perhaps what you require has changed since the last time you thought about it. Regardless of what specific things you come up with, in general, people want comfort, and usually we feel soothed when we feel supported. When you figure out what your spouse could do or say regarding your newfound passion to make you feel comforted or supported, ask for it.

Figuring out what you need and opening yourself up to new challenges makes you more interesting. This will likely increase your confidence, security, and independence. The secret to a thriving marriage is no matter how self-sufficient you are, you always make your spouse feel like he or she has something special to offer you.

Karen and Tom

Karen took decisive steps to figure out what she needed when she recognized a threat to her relationship with her husband, Tom. When Karen and Tom were first married, they were intensely attracted to each other and spent many evenings making love. As the years went by, though, she became less enamored with her life with Tom. An artistic spirit, Karen had often thought of going back to painting, but she was so busy she didn't feel like she had time to spare for it. They usually spent their evenings parked on either side of the couch, watching TV with one eye and their computers with the other. She was also less charmed by Tom himself. The obsession with football she once found so adorable seemed intrusive now that it appeared as if this was the only thing he wanted to do on weekends. They still had sex sometimes, but she thought of it more as maintenance than anything else.

One day Karen talked to a new coworker and was surprised to find out that he was a fan of one of the same contemporary artists she was. They started spending lunch hours together talking about art school or the last exhibit that he had attended and that she had seen advertised in the papers but had missed. Karen was quite self-aware and as she sensed how attracted she was to this man, she realized she needed to do something quickly before she had an affair.

She started begging off lunches with her coworker, choosing instead to take a noontime art history seminar at the local college not far from her office. She looked forward to the class and it became the highlight of her week. She added studio painting after work. She'd come home almost giddy from the high she'd experienced while working on her pieces in class. Tom seemed a bit surprised but was otherwise quiet about her new activity. It wasn't until she overheard his side of a conversation with her father-in-law on the phone that she realized how well he understood what she was getting out of the class: "Yeah, Karen's painting again. What do you mean why? So what if she's not going to be a professional, she loves it!" She was touched. It felt like he was defending her.

Step 3: Affirm Your Partner

What Karen was feeling in that moment was a sense of affirmation. When we choose to change, we are in control. When our spouse changes, however, it can make us anxious. If your partner is the one pursuing new activities, and you're feeling left behind, make an effort to validate her anyway.

One way to manage your anxiety and to protect yourself from feeling left out of your partner's life is to affirm her. Just as you would want support from your partner if you were the one trying to better yourself or learn something new, you need to offer that support. Research has shown that the more a couple promotes each other's goals, the stronger their mutual desire becomes. It's a form of indirect negotiation that's been dubbed the Michelangelo Phenomenon, because the act of affirming a person is akin to shaping material into an ideal figure, much the way the famous sculptor might have created the figure of David from a marble block. Close partners "sculpt" each other in ways that help each to attain his or her goals, ensuring no one gets left behind.

You want to sustain your partner as she strives to become the person she dreams of, not try to mold her into the person you wish she would be. You don't even have to wait for her to get started. Do this even if your spouse has not actively decided to pursue a new goal. For example, if you know your wife has always wanted to play the guitar, give her the gift of a guitar or lessons. If she responds by listing the usual reasons why she never played in the first place— lessons are too expensive, she's too busy, she has no privacy and is self-conscious—have solutions ready. Make it as easy as possible for her to take your gift. If she starts and then allows things to get in the way of practicing or making it to her lessons, tell her you miss the sound of her playing. Make it clear that you're happy when she is happy, and that you're willing to do whatever it takes to support her in the activities and interests that bring her joy.

This is an excellent negotiation tactic that results in marriage longevity. Your partner will be grateful that you did not allow her to cave in to her fears or beliefs that her needs are not worth the effort, and you will be more beloved for it.

The more you confirm your partner's dreams, the greater your desire for each other will become. Your partner's excitement will fuel your own, and vice versa. Excitement triggers dopamine and norepinephrine, the hormones associated with romantic love. The person we want to be around the most is the one that makes us feel sexy, confident, and validated. By affirming your spouse, you can easily fill that role. And thus your pact is adjusted to work for the different yet improved people you've each encouraged each other to become.

How to Affirm Your Partner

The following steps can help you back up your partner and rekindle the desire in your marriage.

- Actively listen. Pay attention to your spouse's words, body language, and behavior. These things will give you a clue as to the ideal person they'd like to become.
- Act according to their needs, not yours. Does your spouse experience love through verbal affirmations, physical affection, kind gestures, or a combination of all three? Adjust your affirmation to fit their desires. For instance, if your wife is the verbal type, she'll prefer being told thank you after preparing a delicious meal. You might even want to mention her kindness to a friend or relative within her range of hearing, so she feels publicly recognized. Alternately, if your husband craves physical affection, give him a loving caress when he announces a raise or promotion. When your partner is stressed and exhausted, do the grocery shopping without being told. The more thought you put into your affirmations, the more effective they will be.
- Be authentic. There's an old saying that goes, "The gift without the giver is bare." That's especially true when it comes to praise. Give it from a place of genuine admiration and desire to support your spouse. Otherwise, it falls flat.
- Be patient. It takes time to earn someone's trust. Don't be surprised if your new behavior is met with suspicion rather than delight. It might take a while for your spouse to believe that your efforts are sincere; sometimes your hard work might only highlight just how absent or disinterested you've been, triggering an increased sense of victimization and outrage. Be respectful of the transition period from end to new beginning. If your first affirmation doesn't go over well, remain calm. Look for another opportunity to support your partner. Consistency is critical. Your behavior will change his behavior. By continuing to give your partner positive feedback, he will eventually let down his defenses and accept your praise and appreciation.

Tom Affirms Karen

The coworker Karen had been attracted to moved to another company, but she continued to enjoy painting and attending museum outings with new friends she made though school. One day she brought home one of her paintings. As she placed it facedown against the wall in her closet, her husband came in.

"Let me see," he said.

"No, it's not that good," said Karen.

Tom came closer. "I'd really love to see your work if you'd let me," he said in a tone she didn't recognize.

Shyly, she turned the painting around. Tom's face lit up. "Honey, this is really good!" She was surprised at how warming it felt to see Tom's admiration and pride. From then on, she shared all of her work with Tom, and sometimes asked him to join her and her friends at the galleries to show him things she thought he might appreciate. He demonstrated so much interest in what she was doing, and so clearly enjoyed spending time with her, that she didn't resent it anymore when he devoted a few hours watching the game on Sundays. Their lovemaking became more frequent, and now it wasn't just upkeep. When Karen saw herself through Tom's admiring eyes, she felt beautiful.

Tom and Karen's old contract had gotten stale and turned them into Ma and Pa Kettle. When Karen reintroduced art into her life, she also introduced a spark of beauty into her relationship. The flame grew as they visited galleries and went to restaurants, and finally made its way into the bedroom.

Renegotiating Through Transition

Maybe you're frustrated because you're seeking out new experiences to make yourself more desirable, but your spouse does nothing in return. Maybe he's resentful of your efforts, or he's refusing to branch out beyond his routine, so not only is he not affirming you, he's not even giving you an opportunity to affirm him back.

If your spouse's transitional period is taking longer than you imagined, whatever you do, don't nag. The only person you can control is yourself, so do the best you can and show enthusiasm for what you're doing. You might need to be patient, but if you consistently make it clear that, while you love the results of your efforts at self-improvement, you'd love it even more if your spouse would support you or participate with you, then he or she will probably come around. If he were showing interest it would mean you were giving him the right amount of space and being open. If he is defensive and angry, you need to understand why. Perhaps in your attempt to include him you've actually become a bit of a nag. By negotiating you can get to the root of the problem and help him feel better. For example, to determine if you are approaching him correctly you could ask, "Do you feel comfortable with my new interest?"

If the answer is, "No," ask, "What is bothering you about it?"

Then listen and keep asking questions until you get it. Repeat what you heard until he says, "Yes, you understand." Then build a bridge between his feelings and yours. For example, if your partner admits to feeling abandoned since you started training for your first triathlon, you could say something like, "I now understand that all the time I put into my training makes you feel like there is no room for you in my life. I feel terrible about that because the whole reason I want to get stronger is so I can be around for a long time. Dying early on you would be the worst way I could abandon you. I love you so much I want as much time as possible with you, and this new hobby is designed to help me stay with you for a long, long time."

If you ask, "Do you feel comfortable with my new interest?" and the answer is, "Yes," ask, "Is there anything not appealing to you about it?"

Listen until you get it. Repeat what you heard until he says, "Yes, you understand." For example, if your partner finally admits, "I'm happy that you're challenging yourself but I don't like feeling left out," you should not consider stopping your activity. Rather, you might say, "I'm really sorry you feel that way and I want to do what I can to fix the problem. Why don't we come up with a way in which you can participate? I'd love it if you helped me train." The point is to show your willingness to make room for your partner in this new part of your life. It may take a few tries, but just making the effort will go a long way toward diffusing any resentment he or she may feel.

Step 4: Assume Nothing

It's possible that you're working with some outdated assumptions or expectations about your spouse, too. You might find that success comes easier if you address them before trying to renegotiate your contract of desire. Take these two steps to make sure you are not working with outdated ideas:

1. Articulate your assumptions.

Maybe you believed that your original unspoken agreement was that your spouse would always bring you a cup of coffee in bed before you got up for the day. It was a sweet gesture she'd always done, and had become part of your implicit contract: "My morning will usually begin with a cup of coffee brought to me by my lovely wife." But over time the coffee stopped coming, and you miss it. You've hinted as much, but the coffee carafe just sits silently on the warming plate of the coffee maker that you preset the night before. Your assumption is: "My wife doesn't care about me enough to bring me coffee anymore."

2. Figure out if your assumptions are true.

The question is, does the fact that your spouse hasn't brought you coffee in bed in years really mean that she no longer cares enough about you? Or is it possible that work is more demanding now and she's more tired, and so has sacrificed the time for an extra ten minutes in bed in the morning? Or could there be some reason you haven't even thought of? The only way to find out is to ask. Failing to discover whether one's assumptions are true or not is a classic mistake people commit in negotiations. It causes them to leave a lot of value on the table. Don't make that mistake when you're trying to renegotiate the most important relationship in your life.

You can garner huge gains in your rapport simply by taking these two steps before ever trying to talk to your spouse about your concerns. The mere attempt to identify which of your assumptions may or may not be true will do you good by automatically making you more open-minded and more aware what your partner might be thinking. Now you're ready for step five.

Step 5: Negotiate to Find a Solution

Often when desire reenters a marriage, one person just started doing his thing, the other one noticed and appreciated it, and yearning naturally starts to flow again. This is the most subtle and elegant of all negotiations. But sometimes we need a more obvious negotiation to get on the same page.

Find a time when you and your spouse are feeling comfortable together, and lay the situation out. Maybe you want to start having children, or your kids are leaving home, or you feel there is distance between you. Regardless, say something along the lines of, "I love you, and I want to plan the next stage of our life as a couple. I want to be your partner in more than just bill paying and dish washing. Could we come up with something to do together?"

Together, make a list of twenty ideas and uncover something that gets you excited. If your spouse seems interested in your least favorite activity, try it anyway. You can always find other things to do together later. "Hey, honey, thanks for letting me help you build that boat. I can't believe how much fun that was. You know what else would be fun? Learning to dance the tango. What do you think?" With all the goodwill and camaraderie and desire built up from all that boat building, it's more than likely your spouse will be willing to try something he might have previously resisted, just because you asked and he wants to make you happy.

Supporting Your Spouse ———————————————

When you recognize and champion your spouse's dreams, you become an integral ingredient to their success. Consequently, their desire for you deepens, because they associate you with personal achievement.

New ideas, adventures, events, and friends can trigger feelings of romantic love between a couple. You might stay together for material ease, security, and comfort, but desire is what will provide the additional sweetness that draws you back for bonus servings of each other.

Chapter 3

Physical Changes: Loving the One You're With

One of the most common reasons couples say that they find it hard to uphold their original contract regarding sex or desire is due to physical changes they undergo over the years. Your wife's raven hair becomes streaked with silver; your husband's jaw merges with his neck. For many of us, age brings more maturity and mellowed standards, so though few people celebrate the arrival of bald spots, weight gain, or decreased agility, aging also often allows us to become more accepting of our own imperfections and those of our loved ones. But some just can't accept these changes, and even find them unattractive.

Couples can also become disenchanted when they witness changes in their partners brought about by illness, injury, or pregnancy. Regardless of why their partner's appearance alters, without the bodily attributes that were once such a powerful draw, some people become less compelled to be physically affectionate, and even have difficulty becoming sexually aroused.

Steps to Renegotiating Through Physical Change

When your dissatisfaction with your partner's physical appearance risks compromising your sex life and, by extension, your relationship, a renegotiation is definitely in order. The following steps can help you accomplish that renegotiation.

Renegotiating Self-Acceptance

You'll get nowhere asking your spouse to make adjustments if you're not willing to make a few yourself. Often when we are asking our partner to change, we are actually reacting to parts of ourselves that we cannot accept. The classic example is when a man trades in his wife for a younger model. It's not that his wife looked so terrible or even so old; it's that she reminds him of his own age, impending frailty, and mortality. Finding a younger wife eases fear temporarily, but of course it doesn't solve the problem—as the younger wife starts to age, the fear will return and the whole cycle will repeat itself. That's no way to live.

Men and women can fall prey to this tendency to project their discomfort with themselves onto their spouses, so it's important to make sure you are in touch with yourself and find pleasure in who you are instead of who you were. Taking the path to self-acceptance will also help in figuring out exactly what it is that you need to ask of your partner. It will also ensure that if you do proceed to ask your partner to make physical changes, it's in his best interest, not just yours.

This step, by the way, is the longest of all the steps in the process of renegotiating physical changes.

Howard and Sophia

Howard was terrified that he would become a cliché because, though he was madly in love with Sophia, he took great pride in her considerable beauty. She was a real head turner. Howard was proud to take her to parties, fundraisers, and work gatherings. Although Howard wanted to marry Sophia, he was afraid that his desire for her would wane as she got older. What if he cheated? He didn't think he could ever admit his concern to Sophia or anyone else, for that matter. He was sure it made him seem superficial and vain. But he also knew that if he ignored his feelings and married her anyway he could bring disaster on both of them.

The most useful strategy for renegotiating self-acceptance is meditation. Tapes, teachers, and retreats can all aid in this journey. Meditation leads to self-love, self-love leads to loving the other, and loving the other leads to fulfillment. With fulfillment comes self-acceptance. Another way to know more about who you are is to get in touch with your sensuality. There are several ways you can do this.

1. Strengthen your mind-body connection.

Activities like yoga, Pilates, guided imagery, fantasizing, masturbation, dance, and deep breathing are all great ways to strengthen your mind-body connection. Tune the world out and focus your attention inward. How do you feel? Where do you carry stress? What hurts? Do you notice an improvement after a certain activity that you enjoy? Start regularly checking in with your body. Listen to what it tells you. The more attuned your mind is to your body, the easier it will be to articulate what you want when you renegotiate with your spouse.

2. Pinpoint what turns you on.

Pay attention to your sexual impulses. If you notice yourself fantasizing about a coworker with a great body, take note. What is it specifically that you like? Did you once love this detail about your spouse, too? Enjoy looking, allow it to turn you on, then go home and jump into bed with your partner. This will help bring the two of you closer. Of course there are differences between what you want and what you have, but there are also pluses to what you have. How has your partner changed in a positive way? Focus on these improvements.

3. Judging yourself is disempowering.

There's no need to carry guilt for being turned on by big breasts, beautiful faces, or fantastic physiques. Honor your feelings. Imagination is sexy. When you feel that way, bring your awakened sensuality into the bedroom. You can enjoy your fantasies and even integrate some of them into your sex life in a way that enhances rather than diminishes your experiences with your spouse. So long as they stay within the boundaries of fantasy, your flights of imagination and thoughts about other people is no threat to your relationship.

4. Experiment.

What felt good when you were first married can change. Injuries and other shifting experiences can interfere with the ability or desire to partake in habitual lovemaking positions. Take this opportunity to mix things up and expand your repertoire. Your spouse may respond so enthusiastically and your lovemaking might improve so much that you'll no longer see a need to ask your partner to change a thing.

5. Be realistic.

If you wish your significant other would do a little more to prevent his or her age from showing, you need to make sure that you can accept that no matter what he tries, he'll never look like the college kid you fell in love with at first sight at his sister's birthday party. It's not fair to ask the impossible of someone.

Howard Renegotiates with Himself

By taking the time to evaluate his fears and find a path to self-acceptance, Howard came to understand that his feelings about Sophia's beauty had more to do with his concern about losing his own youthful looks—he felt she should have been out of his league—and thus would utimately leave him. Eventually he decided to take the plunge and ask her to marry him. He knew that as long as they both stayed comfortable in their own skin, even when they turned 102 they would always see the lovers they are now when they looked at each other.

Focus on the Right Things ————————————

Concentrating on how you feel fuels self-love; concentrating on how you look fuels self-doubt. When you are more forgiving of your physical flaws, it's easier to embrace other people's.

Accepting yourself doesn't mean you can't take steps to improve what you'd like to change, it just means that you're going to harbor realistic expectations and it ensures that no matter how you look, you still like yourself. You can be unhappy with your cellulite or potbelly and determined to do something about it, yet still feel good about yourself.

In many cases, once you've undergone self-evaluation, you'll find that you're no longer bothered by the changes you see in your spouse. There are instances, though, when the alteration that has occurred threatens your health or your value system. A man who feels smothered every time his wife lies on top of him to make love, or a woman whose husband's weight is affecting his ability to get an erection, can't simply accept the transformation. Yet you will violate your marriage contract if you can't find within you a constructive, kind way to encourage your spouse to change. Besides, he will not be open to anything you say unless he can experience the love you intend to convey.

Articulate Your Needs

Once you can put down in black and white what you need, you'll know what compromises you are able to make and which ones you cannot. It's important to know this information before you start negotiating with your spouse or you're likely to agree to something that you'll later regret.

Madeline and Jim

Madeline was distraught because her husband Jim had stopped wanting to make love. Their sex life was fine when they first married, but now Jim complained that sex was painful because of his undescended testicle. Despite the pain and the toll it was taking on their sex life, he was unwilling to get help. Yet Madeline wanted a baby; and a sexless marriage was not an option. She was ready to give him an ultimatum: he would get help and resume sexual relations with her, or she would have to leave the marriage.

Madeline's strategy so far for getting Jim to accede to her wishes had simply been to demand, over and over, that he go to a urologist. She had tried threats, bribes, and begging. What she hadn't tried was negotiating with him and articulating her needs.

With the help of a therapist, Madeline and Jim confronted this issue. Here are the steps they took, which can help you:

1. Make a list.

Madeline and Jim sat down together and wrote a list of all the things they needed from each other. The results were surprising.

Madeline's list was relatively short, enumerating a few common issues about which many wives complain, such as that it would be nice if Jim would help out more around the house, and that she wished he would take more interest in her friends. Predictably, the first item she listed was, "I need you to want to grow a family with me." Madeline was shocked and a little dismayed to see Jim's list. It was longer than hers, filling almost a page. Among his needs were,

"I need you to make my family feel welcome when they come visit," and, "I need you to stop telling jokes at my expense when we're out with other people." She had no idea she had hurt his feelings so often, or that he was harboring so much resentment toward her.

2. Prioritize.

Once the couple exchanged their lists and had taken some time to absorb them, they sat down again and created a chart to prioritize what was most important to each of them. That way, they could concentrate on making sure they were each giving the other what they wanted most.

Remember that though just embarking on this kind of exercise with someone you love will make a positive difference in your relationship, change doesn't happen overnight. You might not really feel like giving your partner what he has asked for. Do it anyway. Act, and the feeling will follow. You'll be amazed at how you are rewarded for your efforts.

3. Create a supportive environment.

While you can't control your spouse's actions, you can help create an environment conducive to success. Put yourself in his shoes. Give positive feedback. Criticism will never work if open-minded creativity is what you wish for; he will simply mount his defenses. The need for positive feedback is true whether you're asking someone to make a significant change, or something more superficial. For example, if you were really turned on by the way your spouse wore his hair long at the beginning of your relationship, tell him in a way that makes him want to grow it out for you. You can say something like, "You have such gorgeous hair. I really miss running my hands through it. Would you mind growing it a bit longer for me? I keep wanting to wrap it around my fingers like I used to." Maybe add, "Is there anything I can do for you?" Remind him of tender, sexy moments you have shared in the past and assure him that you'd like to keep instigating new ones.

Negotiating Weight Loss

Growing out your hair is a pretty simple thing to do, but as most of us know there are other bodily shifts that are exceedingly difficult to avoid or turn around once they set in. Excessive weight gain is one of the most common physical changes people go through, and one of the most distressing, both to the person putting on the pounds, and on occasion, for his or her spouse as well.

To address this delicate issue, wait for the right moment. Your partner should be dressed, relaxed, and not in a rush. Begin by expressing your love. We are all much more receptive to feedback when it comes from a place of affirmation, rather than anger and resentment. "You mean the world to me, and I'm scared I'm going to lose you if you remain at this weight," or, "I can see how unhappy you are with your reflection in the mirror. I love you no matter what you weigh, but I will do anything you want to help you start to feel better about your body. What if we both began Weight Watchers?" You can be honest, too: "Our sex life isn't what I wish it were. What if we made a pact to get ourselves into the best shape we can and see how our new flexibility spices things up? What's more, let's give each other sexy perks along the journey. I will rub your back two times a week for fifteen minutes. In exchange, can I get equal time for a foot massage?"

In each of these cases, you're not blaming your spouse for allowing the weight to pile on, accusing him of laziness or lack of willpower, or putting the burden of making the change entirely on his shoulders. You are making it clear that he will not be alone in his efforts, and that you are available for any support he needs.

Talk about how in addition to improving your health, staying in shape is a means of enhancing your relationship, and that's something for which you're equally responsible. Tell him that you've been cutting out healthy recipes from your cooking magazines and you hope he'll be willing to try them, or maybe even cook them with you. Suggest taking out a joint gym membership, and pay a little extra so you can get time on the racquetball court together. You don't have to sign up for a marathon, but you can get the ball rolling by taking leisurely walks together. Go swimming at the gym or take bike rides when the weather is good.

Since getting enough sleep reduces one's appetite, make sure to encourage your spouse to get to bed at a decent hour. If it's TV that's keeping him up, set the DVR and make sure you both get into bed by ten. Use the time you would have spent in front of the TV burning off some calories with sex (which will also help you both sleep better) or building intimacy by talking without the distraction of any electronic equipment or screens.

Hard-Core Renegotiation

Sometimes weight gain is a sign of depression, or that the person has given up on himself. You might hear a response along the lines of, "I'm fine with my body, why can't you be?" If this is your situation, try giving your spouse incentive to lose weight, something to replace the pleasure of food or to motivate him to get off the couch. Ask him, "What would I have to give you to make you willing to try losing weight?" Be prepared to follow through with whatever he says. Maybe he'd like to go to the movies every Tuesday, or take a weekend away once a month, or have you take over most meal preparations. Maybe he wants you to quit smoking. Show how willing you are to bend over backwards for him and he may be encouraged to try one more time. If his efforts start paying off, it's possible he'll feel so good he'd continue with the new regimen without your active involvement and cheerleading. Still, do not let up nor look for ways to alter your renegotiated contract. If his weight loss is important enough that it warrants a renegotiation, you're going to need to put as much effort into the challenge as he will.

Renegotiating During Pregnancy

Many women find themselves unusually aroused when they are pregnant thanks to the increased hormones racing through their body. Unfortunately, this increased sex drive can often coincide with a sudden decrease in their partner's sexual attraction to them. Some men find pregnancy titillating, but many can't quite reconcile themselves to their partner's rounder, heavier shape. Or they may irrationally fear they are hurting the fetus. Either reaction is normal, but it's important to stay sexually connected during this time.

Both of you may be carrying anxiety about the impending changes a baby will bring to your relationship or your family; connecting physically will go a long way toward easing those concerns. Do everything you can to support your partner's physical needs while she is in this susceptible state, though be sure to let her know if you are feeling vulnerable, too. If she is no longer comfortable with sex, or if the pregnancy is hurting your ability to get aroused, try offering each other massages or spending more time cuddling on the couch while watching TV. Since much of sexual arousal takes place in the brain and not the body, whispering intimacies, or sending sexy voicemails, texts, or e-mails can help your partner continue to feel desirable. Above all, keep in mind that pregnancy is only temporary, and enjoy thinking about how great it will be when you're both ready to rediscover sex with each other.

Renegotiating After the Baby Comes

As any parent of a newborn will tell you, childbirth is a great way to encourage abstinence for some. Watching his wife push a baby out of her body can dampen a man's desire for intercourse, and mothers often need time to recover physically from labor and childbirth. Both parents frequently require time to regain their emotional bearings. Sometimes one partner takes longer than the other to try intercourse again—she still feels fat, or he feels like her breasts are off-limits. The tension this can cause is the last thing a couple needs when they're already dealing with the fatigue and nonroutine of a newborn.

You don't have to start with actual intercourse to get your sex life raring to go again, though. Simply get back into the habit of being physical with your partner. Sexual conversations, mutual pleasuring, making out—all of these can get you back on track until you're both ready to resume intercourse.

Mothers are often dismayed by how slowly the baby weight disappears, and unsurprisingly, fathers can be, too. It's normal to wish that your wife had her prebaby physique. But if your companion is having trouble getting the weight off, and it's important to you that she keeps trying, take an indirect approach. Rather than waxing nostalgic about your wife's formerly flat belly or sexy legs, express longing for the early days of your courtship: "I really miss dressing up when we go out. It was always so much fun to show you off. How about asking your mother to watch the baby, get a mani/pedi and a new dress, and let me take you out on Friday? You pick the restaurant. And instead of a movie, we'll go dancing. We haven't done that in forever, and we were good on the dance floor. It'll be like old times."

Use one of the most powerful arsenals in your marriage—shared memories—to create a satisfying new phase of your sensual life. Once you help your wife regain confidence and remember what it is like to feel sexy again, you can start building momentum toward helping her execute a fitness regimen through some of the suggestions listed earlier in this chapter. If necessary, this is when you can raise your concerns about the state of your sex life, and ask her to help you rebuild the intimacy you miss.

In the meantime, don't ignore your feelings. Release sexual tension by finding ways of self-pleasuring. Find another sympathetic dad with whom you can share your frustrations so that you don't bottle up your emotions and compound the problem.

A couple's devotion to their child is important, but far more important for the future of the family is that partners make sexual needs a priority.

When You Can't Get What You Want

In some cases, your spouse may not be able, or willing, to change, even when you've made it clear how much it would mean to you if it happened. Since you obviously can't force anyone to do what he or she doesn't want to do, it's up to you to learn how to live with the status quo. There might be times when you feel like you simply can't. When you experience this form of powerlessness, you can be vulnerable to the impulse to regain your power by cheating. Suddenly, the world seems filled with people who appear closer to your physical ideal than the person who sleeps beside you, and you can start to wonder if you would be happier in another relationship. It's perfectly natural to appreciate other people's beauty, but infidelity will surely create more distance between you and your partner, which only heightens your dissatisfaction. Ultimately, trading in your spouse for someone else will mean trading in one imperfect person for another.

Instead, if you ever find yourself tempted to stray, channel your sexual impulse and energy toward your partner. It may feel strange or artificial, but remember: act, and the feeling will follow. Try whispering a fond memory of lovemaking when you're both relaxed. Tell your spouse how turned on you were when you first caught sight of him or her naked. Fondle your favorite part of his/her body and describe how much it pleases you. If you're stimulated by his voice, ask to be told a sexy story. Do you enjoy your partner's scent? Breathe deep as you nuzzle his neck or run your fingers through her hair. Stay focused on your sensations, rather than your expectations. You will probably find yourself surprised and delighted at how quickly your body remembers how much it enjoys being with your partner.

Appreciate the Trade-Off

The couple who can be honest with each other in a gentle, constructive manner about what's working for them and what needs to be altered will often find that the new contract that results is stronger and more satisfying than the original ever was. There is little more comforting and satisfying than the security gained from a long-term affiliation. Just because your partner's breasts, abs, or pecs were a major draw when you first met, and they're not anymore, doesn't mean you can't reignite the passion you once felt.

With age comes a slower metabolism, gray hair, and varicose veins, but often it also brings wisdom, perspective, maturity, and strength. Regardless of how we change over the years, those qualities are what make us truly beautiful.

Chapter 4

Nonsexual Gestures of Affection: Loving with No Strings Attached

Though sex is a crucial part of marriage that warrants continuous renegotiation, nonsexual gestures of affection are equally important. In fact, if you're in the midst of negotiating a transition in your relationship, increasing your nonsexual demonstrations of love will help. You'll be amazed at how they calm rough marital waters, and how much easier they make it to connect with, relate to, and resolve conflicts with your spouse. They help your partner feel loved and accepted without judgment.

As an added bonus, you'll find your relationship becomes richer and deeper when you use the techniques suggested in this chapter, all of which encourage you to satisfy your spouse without demanding anything in return.

It doesn't take much to make someone feel loved:

- Offer flowers. This is a popular choice because it works—the gesture actually triggers a positive physiological response.
- Make your spouse's favorite dish from childhood.
- Do your partner's chores when he or she is swamped without waiting to be asked and even without mentioning it.
- Listen to your spouse with intense interest.

Love can be demonstrated in a variety of ways, as listed in Gary Chapman's *The 5 Love Languages*:

- Verbal affirmations
- Gentle touches
- Quality time
- Gifts
- Acts of service
- Kind gestures
- Considerate behavior

On the surface, these actions seem so simple. Why is it so hard, then, for some couples to remember to incorporate these gestures into their daily interactions?

Just as the newness of any relationship fades, familiarity can often breed a sense of entitlement. The breakfast your husband makes you on Sundays, the way your wife picks up the dry cleaning on her way home—it can be easy to take these indirect expressions of love for granted. It's often not until they've disappeared that you realize how much they meant, and by then, unfortunately, whatever caused the other person to stop making the effort is frequently entrenched. And so, just as you must renegotiate to reinvigorate your sex life, and to expand your horizons in the interest of keeping desire alive, you must be vigilant over the implicit contract that dictates how you show love to each other, and renegotiate when necessary.

Three Steps to Renegotiate How You Give and Receive Affection

You can make sure you get the affection you need and not take each other for granted by doing the following:

1. Ask for the affection you want.

If you don't feel appreciated by your spouse, or that he's no longer in tune with what you want, stop and consider what he could do to make you feel loved. Do you like to be complimented or do actions speak louder than words? Are gifts important to you? Do you want more quality time together? Would you like to be cuddled and kissed without feeling pressured to make love? Be specific so you can give valuable pointers when the time is right. Remember, your spouse isn't a mind reader.

2. Express affection.

You may think you are effusive and demonstrative enough, but don't get complacent. Take stock of how you express affection outside the bedroom, and check out if this is what your spouse needs. When your husband's parents announce they are coming to visit, take the opportunity to buy fluffy new guest towels and a bathmat. Show him how nice the bathroom looks, saying, "I thought your parents deserved to feel like coming to see us was a real holiday. Look, I even put a flower in the vase they gave us for our wedding on the dresser." He may appreciate your thoughtfulness as much as your in-laws might.

You could suggest to your wife that she bring home the friends she always talks about from work. Enjoy getting to know them while serving the group drinks and let them socialize while you whip up a lasagna and some garlic bread; then take your plate to the TV room and leave them to schmooze. When you buy yourself a smoothie after your workout, pick one up for your husband. Offer to give your spouse a scalp rub with nothing expected in return.

When you suggest or simply do these small, thoughtful gestures, take note of the other's reaction. If she doesn't seem particularly pleased, find out if there is something else she would prefer. Give with no strings attached. More likely than not, you will find yourself on the receiving end of similar expressions of kindness and love.

3. Acknowledge the affection you receive.

Even when some of the nice things your husband or wife does for you become routine, remember to show gratitude. Return a kindness with a kiss, a smile, or a touch to indicate that you still notice and appreciate his or her thoughtfulness.

Renegotiate How You Express Your Appreciation

Many couples who come to therapists for help consist of a stay-at-home parent and a working spouse. The wife usually pleads exhaustion, the husband often feels rejected and neglected. Regardless of who stays home, it's common for each to believe the other has the easier lot and takes their contributions and sacrifices for granted. To get a couple like this back on track, both need to relearn how to give and receive gratitude and affection.

Often, the best way for this pair to start renegotiating is for the work-outside-the-home parent to make nonsexual gestures of affection without expecting gratification in return. Why should it be this partner who makes the first move? Domestic tasks are notoriously thankless, and by acknowledging that fact and doing one's best to ease some of that burden, a spouse will make him-or-herself more alluring. You'd be surprised at how little it takes to make a tired parent feel like a god or goddess.

Here are some steps you can acquire to renegotiate how you express your affection:

1. Your turn at bat.

Take note of the tasks your spouse hates to do. Laundry, grocery shopping, unloading the dishwasher, chauffeuring the kids around, cleaning the bathroom—managing a household involves a myriad of tiresome daily jobs. Do the least favorite chore without being asked. Don't announce your contribution or draw attention to it; just do it. You may have to make some repeat performances, but eventually, your spouse will notice that you have lightened the load.

2. Give thanks.

Be more mindful of what your partner does for you. Your dry cleaning doesn't just magically appear in the closet. Meals don't prepare themselves. It isn't easy corralling kids into the car and taking them to school every morning. These jobs may not seem arduous to you, but rest assured you would be singing a different tune if they were suddenly loaded on your to-do list. Keep in mind that people perform these jobs out of love—nobody would do this work for a stranger unless paid for it. Take a few moments to notice and acknowledge how your partner makes life easier. At first, your expression of gratitude may be met with suspicion or even hostility— you have unilaterally renegotiated an implicit contract that said you will take each other for granted. Reiterate your sincerity. Continue to do so until your spouse lets down his or her defenses and accepts your thanks.

The advice is the same if you're the stay-at-home parent, by the way. If your partner works to support you, tell him or her you are grateful for the sacrifice, and recognize how hard a person has to work to keep a family fed, clothed, and comfortable.

3. Give each other the gift of free time.

If you can, offer to pay for an occasional cleaning service or babysitter when your stay-at-home spouse reaches the end of his or her rope. Send her to a spa or him to a ball game when the pressure becomes too much. Take the kids to the park Saturday morning so she can sleep in and have privacy for a few hours. When your husband looks exhausted at the prospect of another birthday party, offer to take the children without making a big production of it.

4. Don't expect an immediate return on your investment.

When it comes to gestures of affection, consistency is key. The first time you take over a dreaded chore, your partner may not thank you if he or she is carrying resentment from doing the same job all the time and never being thanked. But by demonstrating your willingness to lighten the load again and again, you'll see the resistance thaw. Eventually, your spouse may explore ways to make your life easier. Best of all, when you turn to each other for sex, it will be out of genuine desire rather than a sense of duty.

5. Develop sacred, sensual rituals.

A marriage that creates a protective cocoon around a duo will serve as a shield against stress and other life pressures. But as most people know, it's easy for couples to get swallowed up by tension and take it out on those they love. You can get so frenzied as you race to keep up with your busy life that you forget to slow down and actually spend time together. That's why, when you're renegotiating the parameters and structure of your marriage—how you show affection in particular—it's important to schedule in a weekly time to share a sensual ritual.

This is not the same thing as date night. Date night is about enjoying activities and public time together. A sacred, sensual ritual is different; it can be something that brings the two of you quietly together, like a bath, listening to music, even dancing. The idea is to spend time together without distractions so you can focus exclusively on each other. A simple ritual that can make a massive difference in how much you communicate can be to schedule one hour a day with all the electronic equipment turned off—no mobile devices, laptops, or televisions allowed. Merely sitting together and listening to each other breathe can be an intimate strategy to start to feel close again.

Goals in Marriage

As Tina Seelig noted in her 2009 *Psychology Today* article, "Mastering the Art of Everyday Negotiations," a key to successful negotiation is to identify a shared goal, which in this case is to have a loving marriage that supports a peaceful, productive, financially secure home life. Consider renegotiating your original contract about whether both partners will work or whether one will work and the other will stay home. Is it time to alter that arrangement? Is it still satisfactory? It's possible that your financial situation requires no changes, or the transformations you'd like to make aren't feasible for the moment, but merely having the conversation that allows you to mutually arrive at this conclusion will help you feel that your needs and concerns are taken seriously. This can be a great strategy for reopening the lines of communication and affection.

More Tips on Building Intimacy

For more great examples of how to show love, we can look to those married couples who are happy and in love, and do not have sexual relations. The individuals in these arrangements are gifted at showing love and creating intimacy in imaginative, meaningful ways. There is no reason any pair can't adopt their techniques.

Sam and Belinda

Sam and Belinda are a married couple in their sixties with three children. Sam is a jovial man whose wife, kids, and friends bask in his unconditional love. Belinda, a wonderful woman in her own right, is a successful accountant with experience evaluating assets. She is aware that her most precious possession is her marriage and treats it accordingly. Whenever Sam gets a professional accolade or is published in an academic journal, she spreads the news with the enthusiasm of a town crier.

Sam and Belinda have not had sex in years due to Sam's impotence. Yet anyone who comes into contact with them can feel the intense connection they share. How are these two able to maintain a loving bond without relating sexually? Because they know how to express affection for each other in a variety of meaningful ways that made both feel valued, special, and appreciated.

For many couples, a lack of sexual intercourse is problematic. At least one partner needs the physical intimacy of lovemaking to feel fulfilled. For Sam and Belinda, though, it isn't a problem. Belinda satisfies her sexual urges through masturbation, and when she wants to be held, kissed, or caressed, Sam is happy to oblige. He is a physically demonstrative man, and enjoys being able to touch his wife in a way that is exclusive to their marriage.

In addition, the couple always verbally affirms each other. This is especially important for Sam, who never got much praise as a child. His mother, an appearance conscious woman, was preoccupied with Sam's tendency to put on excess weight and overlooked his considerable intellectual accomplishments. But Belinda makes it her mission to praise Sam whenever possible. Her eagle eye for detail makes her especially good at pinpointing exactly what makes Sam unique, so her compliments are especially uplifting. Instead of telling him, "Great job!" Belinda will say, "I am so impressed at how you handled Craig at that party. He can be such an obnoxious drunk, but you knew just what to say to make him calm down and stop insulting the hostess."

After many years of marriage, Sam understands how important it is for Belinda to get his undivided attention, so when she comes home from a busy day at work, he makes sure to put down what he's doing and focus solely on her for a short while. Sometimes he'll entertain her with funny stories from his job, or describe a book or movie he read about that might interest her. When the weather is good, he'll invite her to take a walk. He intentionally devotes time to replenishing her emotional well.

What Can You Learn from Sam and Belinda?

Sam and Belinda have mastered the art of showing nonsexual affection. These are some of the things they do well, and how you can use them in your own relationship:

1. Touch your spouse.

Take every opportunity to touch your spouse. Kiss your partner on the cheek as you pass him while he's brushing his teeth; give him a playful hip bump as you head to the fridge when he's at the counter chopping vegetables; hold his hand when you're driving in the car.

2. Compliment with specifics.

Be specific when you offer your partner praise or a compliment. Rather than telling him, "You look nice," try saying, "I love the way that shirt brings out the blue color of your eyes." When he calls you over to see the newly planted begonias, add to the expected, "Very pretty, honey," a little bonus: "It makes me proud every time I see someone admire the front of our house when they walk by. After all the hard work you've put into making it beautiful, you could start a landscaping business on the side. But please don't, I could lose my weekends with you."

3. Focus on each other.

Take a few minutes every day to focus exclusively on each other. If you have to stick to a child's dinner-bath-book-bed schedule, join your wife in the kitchen while she throws dinner together so you can talk. Better yet, rather than split up in opposite directions after the kids are in bed—one person to do dishes, the other to catch up on e-mail—spend a half hour together talking while cleaning up or, if possible, just sitting together on the couch and sharing a cup of tea and a recap of the day. Build quiet daily breaks to share.

Experiment and Take Notes

Keep in mind that not everyone has the same idea of what the perfect expression of fondness looks like. Your husband may shun public displays of affection, but respond well to praise. Some people prefer to be complimented in a private setting, and others enjoy being lauded publicly, such as at parties and dinners. Many people think actions speak louder than words, and are delighted when their partner clears his or her schedule for a romantic weekend. Some spouses are indifferent to gifts and special occasions, and others place tremendous importance on them. Be sensitive to how your companion experiences love, and fine-tune your behavior to match.

Adjust Your Style

You may not feel comfortable with physical displays of affection, but if your spouse thrives on them, someone needs to shift. Consider how you would feel if your significant other withheld a form of warmth that was important to you. Hold hands with your partner. Offer a lingering hug. Run your fingers through his or her hair. You may feel a little ridiculous at first, but after you see how much happiness your efforts engender when you lead the way to the dance floor at a wedding instead of waiting to be dragged out, you'll be glad you tried. As with all new things, practice makes perfect. Eventually the pleasure of seeing your partner's happiness will override any original hesitation or discomfort.

Overall, better results ensue by tailoring your expressions of love in a manner your partner can receive comfortably than by forcing him or her to accept your gestures of affection. Besides, accepting your spouse and affirming his or her uniqueness is one of the most powerful expressions of love there is.

Chapter 5

Trust: Forgiving Extramarital Affairs

For many people, cheating is a deal breaker, the ultimate violation of the marriage contract. It's the one thing a great number of couples swear they couldn't forgive, much less work through. However, studies show that cheating (by one or both partners) occurs in 30 to 60 percent of marriages, which makes it unfortunate that so many people believe they would be incapable of trying to renegotiate following an affair. Marriages can be saved if a couple is willing to find the strength to take the long view and recognize that sometimes a crisis can be the perfect catalyst for negotiating a better, more fulfilling relationship.

Confront the Crisis

Darwin identified two engines that drive evolution: random mutation and natural selection. But there is a third: cooperation. In their book *SuperCooperators*, Martin A. Nowak and Roger Highfield convincingly argue that survival of the fittest is also survival of the most cooperative. Of all the cooperative groups a person can join, the family is the one most conducive to happiness, prosperity, and survival.

Marriages and families work best, however, when members display warmth and acceptance without judgment. If you withhold compassion from your spouse after discovering infidelity, or reject compassion when it's offered, you create yet another barrier and make it even harder to improve your marriage.

When cheating is revealed, it's natural for people to vent feelings of anger, hurt, and betrayal, but if you hope to renegotiate trust, confronting your spouse with endless bitterness or rage is debilitating for both of you. Pushing him or her farther away encourages even more withdrawal and abandonment. When met with compassion, warmth, and a sincere desire to learn why the betrayal occurred, however, a cheating spouse might be reassured that cooperating to rebuild the marriage will not result in a lifetime of guilt trips and perpetual distrust, but an existence of increased fulfillment, security, comfort, and safety.

Though the causes of affairs tend to be shockingly predictable, the renegotiation path every couple must take will be unique. Yet as you will see in the two following examples of various negotiation techniques, successful renegotiations through infidelity have two things in common:

1. The betrayed spouse did not verbally or emotionally attack his partner
2. The cheating spouse underwent an intense journey of self-discovery

Allie and Ben

Allie, a high-ranking bank executive, grew up in an intensely religious household and went to Catholic school all the way through college. While she had a deep faith, her upbringing had led her to stifle any exploration of her wild, whimsical side. In addition, she was shy and self-conscious. She and Ben met when they were young, in their early twenties. They were an excellent match. Ben was quiet and conservative but supportive of Allie, and they shared a great deal in common. With Ben, you always knew what to expect, and he made Allie feel safe. While some of her friends played the social circuit for a few more years after graduating, traveled, or tried on different careers for size, Allie took a job at a bank and settled into a quiet, comfortable domestic and professional routine.

As the years went by, however, she began to feel that she might have missed out, that maybe her family had forced her into a mold not of her own choosing. Lurking beneath her subdued surface, she believed, was an adventurous person that she had never indulged, one she was sure she would never get to explore in her relationship with Ben, who was kind and loving, but whose idea of risk was ordering his hamburger medium rare.

She started working on a project with a coworker named Ken, the polar opposite of Ben—an older, rugged, outdoorsy type who loved ethnic restaurants, read books by foreign authors, and had a devil-may-care approach to life. Allie loved Ben, but she was incredibly drawn to Ken and couldn't resist the opportunity to let her inhibitions loose. She and her coworker started having an affair.

Predictably, the affair flamed out after a few months. Much to her own surprise, however, Allie found herself tumbling into a wild relationship with a younger man in her department. She realized her antics were not only putting her marriage in jeopardy, but her career as well, yet she almost felt powerless in the throes of her desire to explore every aspect of the personality she had so long tried to subdue. In addition, she lived in fear of being found out by her husband. What if another coworker blew the whistle on her?

What she did not know is that her husband Ben was already aware of what was going on. He had long been disappointed in the distance that had developed between him and his wife, but had accepted that it was inevitable for the lusty days of their courtship to become a faint memory. When Allie began her affairs, however, Ben sensed an even greater wall between them. He didn't know the details, but he could read the signs—the increasingly late nights, the whispered phone calls, the hastily shut cell phone. Though he spent many evenings hiding in his office pretending to work while pacing the room as he tried to figure out how to confront Allie, he continued to act as if nothing had changed between them. He did his best to remain what he had always been—calm, supportive, and loving.

Eventually, Allie could no longer carry the guilt of her indiscretion and, shaking with fear, she confessed to Ben. She expected fireworks, a torrent of anger and blame, maybe even an immediate demand that she leave the house. Instead Ben, who after all had already guessed that she was hiding something, said, "Thank you. It's a relief to finally know the truth." He told her that he felt hurt, betrayed, and belittled but that he still loved her and believed their marriage was worth saving. He hoped she would be willing to try to work things out. He urged her to find a therapist, perhaps one they could see together so they would have a safe, neutral place to work out their feelings.

By responding to his wife's indiscretions with authentic pain and sadness coupled with patience and acceptance, Ben prepared the way for renegotiation.

On the other hand, when you feel guilty about how you've treated someone, that kind of response can almost be more difficult to take than anger and rejection. How will you ever feel like you deserve your spouse again? How will you ever rid yourself of the weight of your guilt and sense of responsibility, especially in the face of such kindness?

To Allie, the breach of their contract seemed so harsh it might almost be easier to abandon the relationship than struggle to get through their crisis. She didn't see how she and Ben could work their way back to each other. Yet she still loved Ben, and so in spite of her doubt and shame she did not reject the love that Ben offered her. In this way, she, like Ben, let her cooperative instincts override her impulse to flee.

Four Steps to Renegotiating after Infidelity

If cheating has occurred, you can take some steps to heal your relationship and renegotiate your marriage. One of the first things you'll have to do is override your impulse toward self-flagellation, if you're the adulterer, or your sense of self-righteous indignation, if you're the betrayed spouse. In addition, you may have to fight the urge to incessantly ask detailed questions about the affair. Knowing all the details will not help you, and forcing your spouse to answer your questions will merely torture you both. Rather than sink into this common pitfall, try the following:

Take a Journey of Self-Discovery

Whether you're the person who strayed or the spouse betrayed, do some intense thinking about which of your requests must be met in order to continue your relationship. In addition, you need to know not just who you are, but who you want to become. That knowledge will be the starting point for any negotiation that follows.

Allie did start seeing a therapist, and was told that her dream of having a satisfying romantic relationship with her husband would remain elusive until she became comfortable with the adventurous side of her that had been stifled as a child.

Allie decided to transfer to a more prestigious position within the bank at their London branch. She understood Ben's fear that she was trying to put even more distance between them, but she knew it was the right thing for her, both professionally and personally. For one thing, moving offices allowed her to break all ties with her younger lover. For another, she had never lived alone before, and she was sure that doing so would help her get more in touch with her own wants and needs. The arrangement worked out even better than she could have hoped. It was like she had been looking at herself too closely in a mirror, and had stepped back so she could really see her reflection. Living on her own was exhilarating, but she was delighted to discover that whenever she had a new experience, or a triumph at work, or saw something wonderfully, hilariously British, she felt compelled to call Ben and tell him about it. With some distance, she was able to see Ben for who he really was.

Get Tech on Your Team

Use technology wisely. With mobile e-mail, Skype, cell phones, Twitter, and Facebook, you're never really far away from anyone. Even when you've got your nose to the grindstone, if your partner crosses your mind for any reason, let him or her know with a brief text, short phone call, a poke, or a tweet without requiring an immediate reply. This small gesture will help build intimacy and closeness, even as you're taking time apart.

Be There

The spouse who has been betrayed has one primary job: show up. And if you truly want your marriage to work, welcome your other half with warmth and acceptance when your partner tries to take steps toward you.

Allie worked intensely for four days a week and would return home to enjoy long, pressure-free weekends with her husband. Usually they spent the time quietly together at home, working on the garden or playing with the dogs. Most important, they talked—about their work, about what they read in the news, about the differences between the United States and the United Kingdom, about anything and everything except Allie's affairs.

Ben wasn't sweeping anything under the rug by avoiding this painful topic. In his mind, what was done was done; rehashing the hows and whos wouldn't help anyone. He was comfortable with who he was, and he knew that he and Allie complemented each other. It was up to her to learn self-acceptance, and to remember why she had married him in the first place. If she could do that emotional work on her own, he was sure she would come back to him, and when she did, he would be waiting.

The strategy worked. Had Allie been afraid that every now and then she would be raked over the coals for her behavior, or that Ben would throw her indiscretions in her face during a disagreement or use them to gain power in the relationship, she never could have faced more years with him. His judgment and condemnation would have made it too hard for Allie to take any steps back to him. His forbearance and forgiveness, however, intensified her motivation to make things work between them.

That doesn't mean Ben didn't suffer or struggle with powerful feelings of rage and sadness over losing Allie twice to two lovers and now to London, but he worked through those emotions in a therapy group and by speaking almost daily to his best friend Charlie.

Breed Desire Through Freedom and Novelty

Inject some of the novelty and excitement that once existed during the early lust and romantic phases of your relationship. In this way, you will take steps toward rekindling the desire you originally felt for each other.

As Ben realized his wife was eager to connect with him, his self-esteem started to soar. One day he surprised her by meeting her at the airport with tickets to a food and wine festival taking place in a town just a few hours away. Together they drove straight from the airport to spend the weekend at a bed and breakfast, eating and drinking themselves into a glorious food coma. Allie couldn't believe that she was with the same Ben who had once said, "Why would I want to sleep anywhere else when I have a perfectly nice bed at home?" She was touched by his thoughtfulness and his effort.

Move Out of Your Comfort Zone

Both spouses need to make adjustments. Life will never be what it was before, but it's possible that if you creatively negotiate, you might find it becomes even better. No one should be expected to be someone they're not, but occasionally it only takes a small shift in behavior to make your partner see you in a new light. If you usually try to talk your husband out of the movie he suggests— "Too violent," "Too scary," "Oh God, another romance?"—next time, just nod and buy the tickets as soon as he tells you what he'd like to see. When you find out her favorite band is coming to town, buy the tickets without telling her, and start learning the lyrics to all those songs she loves. If you're not athletic but you know he'd love to go on a hiking trip, ask him to help you get in good enough shape so you can start planning to do a short hike on the Appalachian Trail. As you make efforts to embrace the things that make your spouse happy, you'll find that your spouse will more often than not move equally quickly toward making you happy as well.

Betty and Thomas

Like Ben, Thomas's strategy for negotiating through his wife's infidelity was to show tremendous self-restraint and patience. He also took a few more steps that couples can consider should they find themselves in a similar situation.

Thomas had seen no reason to object when his wife Betty reconnected on Facebook with her old college boyfriend, Albert, who had moved back to Berlin after graduate school.

Over time, however, he began to notice that she was spending increasing amounts of time at her computer. He could feel Betty begin to retreat from the marriage. She no longer came to bed until he had turned off the light. She preferred to stay in the study, surfing the web, rather than sit in the living room with him to watch TV. Finally, one day he accidentally saw the contents of an e-mail: "I know you're not happy. Come to Berlin. I'll show you the time of your life."

Understandably, Thomas was incensed. He took pride in not being the jealous, possessive type, and this is what he got for it? His impulse was to start divorce proceedings. But after sitting on his emotions for a few days and clearing his head, Thomas started thinking about what divorce would really entail, and the trauma it would cause the children.

A Good Reason to Renegotiate Your Marriage ————

Thomas, a physician, knew something about the well-documented health risks associated with divorce. In her 2009 article, "Marital Biography and Health at Midlife," sociologist Linda Waite documented that, overall, men and women who experience divorce or the death of a spouse report about 20 percent more chronic health problems like heart disease, diabetes, and cancer compared with those who have been continuously married. Getting remarried helps alleviate some of the negative fallout of divorce, such as depressive symptoms, and yet compared with those who have been continuously married, people in second marriages have 12 percent more chronic health problems and 19 percent more mobility problems.

In addition, Thomas was not blind to the fact that he owed many of the comforts and pleasures in his life to Betty. While he worked long hours, she held down the fort at home, playing chef, chauffeur, disciplinarian, tutor, nursemaid, and housekeeper. She kept the chaos at bay. A prudent man, Thomas recognized it might be in everyone's best interest to see if he and Betty could work things out before abandoning all hope for a happy future.

Five More Steps to Renegotiating after Infidelity

As anyone who has given birth or had surgery knows, pain fades over time. At the moment nothing could hurt more than imagining your partner with someone else, but if you commit to your marriage, over the lifetime of your relationship the rosy memories will be the ones to stay while the darker ones will dissipate.

Renegotiating your marriage is worth the effort so you can get to the joy waiting for you on the other side of your mountain of misery. You can try some of these additional tactics to get you through:

Seek Help Within the Community

In many religious wedding ceremonies, the minister, priest, or rabbi will acknowledge the guests who have gathered and remind the bride and groom that these people are all there to support them not just on their wedding day, but throughout their lives. In times of crisis, when trying to determine the best plan to renegotiate trust and encourage cooperation, there's nothing wrong with asking members of your community for help.

Intent matters—it would be wrong to ask someone your spouse trusts to spill his or her secrets. You must make it clear that you don't want to violate anyone's privacy. Your goal is to heal, build bridges, and repair damage, not dig up your partner's secrets to use as evidence against him. Those secrets are meaningless anyway unless you plan on inflicting punishment, which doesn't dovetail with renegotiation.

Thomas turned to his sister Wendy for help. She and Betty had always been close; he'd always joked that Betty might have married him just to make sure she didn't lose Wendy. Delicately, Thomas asked Wendy if there was anything she could tell him that could help him understand what it was that drew Betty to Albert. "I don't want you to tell me her secrets. Can you please just tell me anything that would help me figure out the right way to talk to her about this so she doesn't run straight into that jerk's arms?" Wendy, who already knew about Betty's interaction with Albert, considered herself a trustworthy friend, and wouldn't dream of telling Betty's husband anything that could cause further harm. Instead, she revealed something Betty had told her she wished she could find the courage to tell Thomas herself: Betty was bored and lonely. Though she had two college degrees and could easily have had a stellar career, after the birth of their second child, she and Thomas had decided their children should have their mother at home.

At first Betty was thrilled and grateful for the luxury to be home with her children. But by the time her fourth baby had headed into the terrible twos, motherhood had become a mind-numbing experience. Then Albert appeared, and life moved from black-and-white to Technicolor.

When Albert found her on Facebook, a whole new world opened up. When she talked to Albert, she felt like she was flexing intellectual muscles that were about to atrophy. He paid attention to her, asked her opinion, and made her feel sophisticated and clever. When Thomas came home from the hospital where he worked, he was rarely in the mood to talk. He wanted to roll around on the floor with the children, eat a good meal, watch a little TV, do some work, and get to bed before 10 P.M. His life functioned like clockwork because Betty was always there to make sure it did. But when did he ever do anything for her?

See Through the Other's Eyes

It's easy to forget that the life we experience may look completely different from someone else's perspective. Such tunnel vision can make it very hard to renegotiate, since the process depends on being able to consider another person's point of view. Wendy was able to provide Thomas with the perspective he needed, but not everyone will be so lucky to have someone like Wendy in his life. That's why it's important that you constantly reinforce your sense of empathy and make sure that you occasionally try to put yourself in your partner's shoes.

Through Wendy, Thomas learned that Betty felt that there was an imbalance in the life they had negotiated together. It was probably her perceived sense of unfairness and victimization that led Betty to justify the treacherous path she was heading down with Albert. It's a common occurrence, according to Dr. Anjan Chatterjee of the University of Pennsylvania in a 2011 *New York Times* article "The Psychology of Cheating" by Benedict Carey; once you see yourself as a victim, "it becomes a matter of evening the score: you're not cheating, you're restoring fairness." Betty had become so convinced of her victimhood, she felt almost entitled to the good feelings her relationship with Albert gave her.

With this small piece of information, Thomas now had a better idea of how to approach Betty in such a way that she might be willing to work with him to rebuild their relationship. Thomas asked Betty if she would be open to spending a weekend in Montauk with him. She was shocked at the invitation. At first she demurred, citing the children's sports events, though in reality she was terrified of spending that much time alone with her husband when things were so awkward between them. But Thomas had anticipated this, and had arranged for Wendy to watch the kids if Betty would allow it. Surprised and intrigued, Betty agreed.

The weekend was a cathartic bonding experience for both of them. Not once did Thomas bring up the subject of Albert.

Abandon Your Assumptions

When considering how to approach your renegotiation, make sure to take stock of any assumptions you might carry about your spouse, or why he or she cheated, or how he or she feels about your relationship. Assumptions are the antithesis of empathy, pigeon-holing other people into the little box you've built for them. You have to let them go before embarking on any renegotiation.

Thomas's plan was to spend the weekend getting to know his wife again and learning exactly what she felt she needed to make their current life more vibrant. He and Betty spent hours walking along the beaches with Thomas asking many questions and Betty answering more and more openly and honestly as she understood that her husband had not brought her there to give her an ultimatum or back her into a corner—her own erroneous assumption. Thomas asked a lot of questions, but listened, too. The more he did, the more he started to understand that he had made a lot of guesses about Betty that weren't true, just as she had incorrectly believed that he didn't value her.

In business negotiations, inaccurate presuppositions often lead people to leave a great deal of value on the table. A developer interested in a piece of property might assume that the seller will never agree to help pay to move the historic farmstead located on the land to a new location. Had he asked, though, he would have found that the seller was prepared to do just that, saving him a substantial amount of money.

In relationships, such erroneous assumptions can sabotage any efforts to come to a mutually acceptable agreement. A woman who thinks her husband will never agree to stop attending his obnoxious cousin's weekly cigar and poker party in their grandmother's basement leaves no room to work out a compromise that he will only go every other month and promise to come home sober. Yet if she tried to test her assumption and found out she was wrong, she might be able to release the resentment and frustration that she is letting seep into other aspects of their lives. Inaccurate and untested theories are like the unseen flotsam floating around beneath the surface of the sea that, upon contact, can tear a hole in an otherwise sturdy boat.

Stay Flexible

Adjusting your negotiating style to that of your partner is a crucial way of getting a possibly reluctant negotiating partner to be open about what he or she really wants. Some people are impatient and need to make decisions quickly, others are nitpicky and analytical; many people like to list pros and cons and even sleep on decisions before making them.

Identifying and then respecting your spouse's negotiating style, rather than pressuring her to tailor her style to yours, will help move your conversation forward and craft a positive outcome for both sides.

Thomas, always practical and efficient, would have liked to try a point-blank approach when talking to Betty about what she wanted from their relationship, but as he listened to her, he realized that Betty responded best when she was given plenty of time to turn an idea over in her mind before committing to a reply.

Stay Open to Surprise

It pays to listen closely. Often couples have been together for so long they believe they know everything there is to know about each other, but there is always more to learn. Keep your mind open, keep the conversation going, and let your spouse surprise you. The more time you spend listening, the more surprises you will hear. While sharing a cup of coffee on the balcony of their rented condo, Thomas asked Betty what he could do to show her that he still found her sexy. "You could try to seduce me more often," she murmured into her cup. Thomas was astounded. "You don't get enough sex?" he asked. "You're exhausted all the time! Most of the time when I try to get things started you push my hands off you and tell me you're tired." Betty looked at him shyly. "I said I wanted you to seduce me. Grabbing my behind while I'm brushing my teeth is not a seduction. It doesn't do much to put me in the mood. I don't want sex to be just one more thing to get done like everything else in my day. I want to be romanced and get to anticipate the sex after spending time doing something else."

That's when Thomas realized that Betty wanted to be courted, just like she had been when they were first dating. That's why Albert's advances were so irresistible. Thomas suggested they go out every Saturday night, and dress up just a little even if they were just going to the movies, to make it more fun to undress when they'd end the evening in each other's arms.

Over the course of their conversation, Thomas would find himself surprised one more time. As they walked past a small shop advertising music lessons, Thomas mentioned that he thought their oldest son might be ready to start piano lessons. At this Betty stopped and turned to him, her eyes hard. "Only if you change teachers," she said firmly.

Thomas was baffled. Change teachers? Thomas had been taking piano lessons from a Russian woman for about three years, and had made great progress. His lessons were the highlight of his week. Afterward, his teacher would serve a small glass of port and they would talk for a few minutes about their families, or their favorite composers, or the last movie they'd seen. As it turned out, Betty was jealous.

Thomas reassured Betty that there was absolutely nothing going on between him and the teacher, but since it bothered her, he would start coming home right after the lessons. He did, and that was that.

Thomas would never have known that Betty was harboring resentment about his post-piano-lesson drink if he hadn't paved the way for more open communication. Of everything he heard that weekend, that news was the most surprising.

Why Cheating Is Bad for You

Regardless of how skillfully a couple renegotiates trust, unless the unfaithful partner recognizes what he was getting out of the clandestine relationship, and seeks to create that same element or quality within his own marriage, there exists the chance that he will stray again. It was imperative that Allie and Betty acknowledge that although the initial rush was exhilarating, their affairs did not create personal power or better versions of themselves.

In fact, their affairs were debilitating over the long term. They were making themselves vulnerable, relying on other people to feel good, when they had the power to give themselves that boost all along. Relying on an outsider to provide a stamp of approval is ultimately a weakening act, for it puts you at his mercy. Self-affirmation, although hard to come by for some, is empowering.

Patience in Transition

Besides experiencing the pain and damage of infidelity, these two couples were alike in one other way. When the husbands initiated a renegotiation, they did not spend a lot of time rehashing the details of the affairs that threatened their marriage. Nor did they push their wives to make immediate changes. In both cases, the men exhibited extraordinary patience.

You may have heard of the stages of grief that follow a loss. Similarly, three stages of transition follow any crisis or major change. Finding out that a spouse has been unfaithful is one of the hardest blows you can experience. When you face such a crisis and take the steps to renegotiate trust, it's extremely helpful to keep these stages in mind:

1. The End

This is the time when we grieve for what we've lost, when we rail at the unfairness of life, and when we feel compelled to assign blame. It can be a frightening, disorienting period as we try to regain our emotional footing.

2. The Readjustment

After a while, our emotions inevitably begin to settle and we're able to think a little more rationally about how our life is changing. At this point, people often feel like they're in limbo. They accept that things cannot stay the same, and they take tentative steps to move beyond the immediate crisis, but they're not quite sure how things are going to look in the future.

3. The New Beginning

For everything we mourn, there is always a new beginning. At this stage, people are ready to reinvent themselves, branch out, take risks, and accept change. Too often, the slow pace of transition frustrates people and they give up midway through the process, choosing instead to seek out a new beginning with a new partner. This is unfortunate, for the couple that renegotiates trust, and crosses though the three stages of transition together, is inevitably stronger and more resilient than one that never has.

Part 2

Renegotiating How to Honor One Another

As couples move through life together, they are constantly challenged to make decisions that support their individual needs, goals, and dreams, yet also uphold those of their spouses. It's not always easy. You will always have two choices: first, to exert control, or second, to exert influence to get what you want. But the one you choose most often will determine whether you have a calm, harmonious future, or one filled with conflict and struggle. Attempting to control your spouse through threats and emotional manipulations is not negotiating, it's bullying.

To negotiate successfully you must influence your partner by making your needs clear while showing that his or her needs are important to you, too. Showing your partner honor and respect at all times will help you find solutions that will benefit you both and ease the way for every negotiation you embark on together.

Chapter 6

Children: Remaining Lovers After Becoming Parents

"Children are a great comfort in our old age . . . and they help us reach it faster, too." It's a funny line because it's so true. Nothing can infuse a marriage with as much excitement, joy, and fun as the arrival of children. Unfortunately, nothing can infuse a marriage with as much unpredictability, anxiety, and stress, either.

Though our culture's overwhelming message is that children should be the ultimate goal and priority in a marriage, and the source of a couple's greatest happiness, recent research reveals a somewhat darker reality. When demographers Rachel Margolis and Mikko Myrskylä surveyed 200,000 people in eighty-six countries, their data, published in the March 2011 issue of *Population and Development Review*, showed that young couples in their twenties who remain childless are far happier than pairs in their twenties who become parents, and couples in their thirties who proclaim themselves happily married experience a dramatic dip in contentment once their children are born. Only twosomes who procreate for the first time in their late thirties, forties, and even fifties report a consistent level of happiness above what they previously experienced, presumably because they are so grateful to have been able to have children before their biological window of opportunity closed.

Though many people react strongly to such reports—"Anyone who doesn't love every minute with their children doesn't deserve them" and "No one's going to tell me my kids don't make me happy"—these facts don't diminish the importance and value of children and parenthood. Rather, they simply reveal a truth that can be hard to acknowledge: raising kids is hard, expensive, time-consuming, and above all, a romance killer. Children keep couples distracted from the aspects of their relationship that, as we've established, keep a marriage strong—frequent sex, time alone together, shared activities, undivided attention. Whereas before, partners could usually find enough occasions outside of work and other obligations to devote to each other, now that time is spent focusing on the children. In the words of psychologist Daniel Gilbert delivered during a 2010 lecture at the American Psychological Association convention, "Children take lovers and turn them into disgruntled parents." When you add in the pressures of the workplace, especially in a difficult economy, the heightened demands to parent "perfectly," the lack of family support, and the expense of childcare, it's no wonder so many marriages collapse just a few years after children come into the picture.

But they don't have to. Every family with kids will go through short periods of near Rockwellian bliss only to wake up one morning to find they are living a scene out of *Dennis the Menace* or *National Lampoon's Vacation*. No, parenting is not always fun, but it is incredibly fulfilling and rewarding. And it doesn't have to drain the romance and vitality out of a marriage. Those couples who can find a way to negotiate their partnership successfully through the three stages of child rearing—infancy/childhood, adolescence, and young adulthood—can set themselves up for a lifetime of joy and satisfaction once the kids are launched and they are able to focus exclusively on each other again. That's not to say that adult children can't present their own set of challenges; they can sometimes be even more disruptive because parents no longer have any control over them. Yet, they are adults, which means that you can prioritize your needs and your marriage in a way that was more difficult back when they were small.

Infancy/Childhood

As anyone with kids will confirm, the first years of child rearing are some of the most grueling. An infant's or small child's total physical and emotional dependence can be a heavy weight on new parents, and especially mothers. In spite of the phenomenal progress men have made over the last forty years in terms of pulling their own weight at home and being involved, attentive parents, it is still usually mothers who bear the brunt of the daily responsibilities that come with child rearing. Overall, mothers are more often the ones to plan meals, shop for clothes, arrange for childcare, and be involved in school activities and organizations.

It is often during this phase that women begin to feel that they got the short end of the stick back when they originally negotiated having children with their spouse. Weren't they supposed to have married in a postfeminist, egalitarian era? Men, too, can find themselves disappointed in the way their relationship changes once children arrive. Breastfeeding, co-sleeping, and the general 24/7 aspect of infant care can leave a husband feeling like his role in his wife's life has been usurped. Even as the kids get older, his wife might be often so exhausted from taking care of children all day, or juggling the demands of work and family, that asking for sex feels almost like an imposition. Fathers, too, can struggle with the heightened desire to succeed that often accompanies parenthood. The responsibilities and determination to be a good provider can be overwhelming.

The adage that "a baby changes everything" couldn't be truer. Every couple has to renegotiate the relationship once children come into the picture. It's simply impossible to know whether the arrangements you agreed to before each child comes will remain viable once the new arrival becomes part of daily life. A woman might realize that she's just not cut out for stay-at-home motherhood, or a father might discover that his professional ambitions aren't nearly as important as making sure to get home before the kids are in bed. These realizations will have a profound effect on a family. Couples who are quick to renegotiate once they absorb the massive changes present in their relationship, and how much more work it will take to stay connected, can protect and even strengthen their marriage during this challenging yet exhilarating time.

First: Remember the Romance

Once couples become parents, they need to start working at being lovers. It is imperative that parents get out of the house and away from the children at least once a month. If the cost of a babysitter makes this idea prohibitive, start a babysitting co-op in which families trade nights taking care of each other's children. Some churches and synagogues host monthly Parents' Night Out, where kids are dropped off for a few hours so parents can get away. Arrange a rotating movie night with families in your neighborhood. Every Friday the kids descend on one home for two or three hours of pizza, popcorn, and the four thousandth viewing of *Star Wars*, and the other parents enjoy a quick happy hour or even just head right back to the house for some sexual, sensual time in their own bed or bathtub.

Forget Fairness

As responsibilities mount and we scramble to keep up with the pressures of life and our obligations, it's easy for couples to begin a game of tit for tat. "I took the garbage out the last three nights in a row; you can do it for the rest of the week." "You can't go out with your friends now. I had the kids all day." "I'll come upstairs when you're done with story time." "I don't care that you worked late last night, it's my turn to sleep in." People's obsession with fairness in marriage has done in many a good relationship. You have to keep things fluid. At any given time someone is always going to be a little more inconvenienced, do a little more work, get a little less sleep. But you'll achieve a far greater serenity if you can simply roll with the unpredictability of life and let go of the fairness ideal you might have started out with in the early days of your relationship. Who does what, and for whom, and when, generally all evens out over the lifetime of a marriage. The more time you spend together as lovers the less fairness will be an issue, and the more you will each feel appreciated.

Annie and Albert

Sometimes couples are shocked to find that their assumptions about what kind of parent their partner will be, was dead wrong. When Annie was pregnant with her first son, she daydreamed about what a great father her husband Albert was going to be. She had delighted hearing about how her friends' husbands, mostly go-getter business types, had crumbled into sentimental softies when their children were born. She couldn't wait to see this side of Albert emerge, nor could she wait for motherhood.

Four years and another son later, Annie was a walking live wire—stressed-out, passive-aggressive, ready to snap. Her disillusionment about what raising children with Albert would be like was profound. As it turned out, though Albert loved his children and had big plans for them, he didn't really like babies. "I'm hopeless around the helpless," he'd joke. Their crying made him uncomfortable, and he was quick to hand them over to his wife as soon as her hands were free. "He wants you," he'd say as he headed back into the living room, leaving Annie to rock and cuddle her wailing infant. When her second son was born about twenty months after her first, she thought surely Albert would recognize that she needed him to help out more, but though he praised her constantly for what a great job she was doing, he didn't adjust his work schedule so he could come home sooner, nor did he take over any of the household duties. Albert had always needed plenty of sleep to feel at his best, and so during the first few months of both children's lives, Annie slept in the baby's room or on the couch so he wouldn't be disturbed when the children cried out in the middle of the night. When her friends expressed disapproval with this arrangement, she'd reply defensively, "How can he do his job well if he's a walking zombie like me? At least one of us has to get a good night's sleep. It's just temporary. You'll see."

As the children grew from infancy to childhood, however, Annie was dismayed to find that Albert didn't become more interested in taking care of his kids. He talked about how great it was going to be when they were old enough to play baseball and take on camping trips, but he showed no initiative in assuming some of the childcare load, even when she took on an at-home, part-time job handling online sales for a guitar store.

From Albert's perspective, everything was as it should be. He worked hard all day to make sure that his business would provide everything the family could possibly need. He admired Annie's way with the kids and was proud of his little family. He had arranged a standing semimonthly babysitter so he and Annie could go out every other Saturday night together. He always hoped that the evening would end in lovemaking, and sometimes it did, but it always felt like Annie was doing him a favor. More often than not Annie would quickly strip out of her dress, put on her pajamas, and turn out the lights. He'd relax in front of the TV, or sometimes, with Internet porn.

Over time, despite the twice-monthly dates, the tension between Albert and Annie had grown almost impenetrable, and they barely spoke. Annie had tried everything—guilt trips, the cold shoulder, lukewarm dinners, withholding sex—and nothing would make Albert budge from his conviction that he was already doing as much as he could. Albert, frustrated by what he perceived as his wife's ungrateful, entitled attitude, retreated more and more into his work.

The Problem

Annie and Albert both fell into the classic trap that many new parents experience of making assumptions of what parenting will actually be like, and what kind of parents they will be. Even if the hospital sent new babies home with a guidebook, it wouldn't do anything to prepare individuals for how much parenthood will or will not change them. Annie wrongly assumed that Albert would easily adapt to parenthood, and Albert assumed that the arrangement they agreed upon before the children were born would always work.

Rather than adjust their expectations when faced with evidence that the assumptions they'd made were incorrect, they each simply dug their heels in deeper, sure that if they stuck to their original plan, the other would come around. To renegotiate, they'd each need to gain perspective, find empathy, and think creatively about how to adjust their image of the perfect family.

Four Steps to Renegotiating Childcare

People's parenting style often stems from their own life experience. Some people who grew up with absentee parents overcorrect and become helicopter parents; others simply continue the cycle. Adults who had strict parents might be strict themselves, or they might take a decidedly hands-off approach in an attempt to avoid repeating what they see as their parents' mistakes. Renegotiating how you parent requires that you become more conscious of your parenting decisions, so that they are made carefully and thoughtfully, not reflexively in light of your own history. Draw from the best of your experiences, and jettison the rest.

Make a List

When tensions rise over childcare, it's helpful to get a black-and-white view of the situation. One way to do this is to make a list of what you do every day.

Albert and Annie felt unappreciated for what they contributed as parents and providers to their family, so the first thing they had to do was get a clear view of what those contributions actually entailed. They needed to sit down and make a list of everything they did from the moment the boys woke up until they went to sleep.

A sample of Annie's list looks like this:

- Get breakfast for boys
- Clean up kitchen
- Get boys dressed, teeth brushed, etc.
- Take Adam to school
- Take Dylan to gymnastics, Mommy and Me, music, etc.
- Get groceries, dry cleaning, other errands
- Make lunch
- Have story time
- While Dylan naps: clean up kitchen, sweep and vacuum, sort laundry, make sure all ingredients in place for dinner, do work-related tasks such as go through mail, check e-mails, check voicemail, return correspondence, and process orders
- Prepare snack time
- Pick big boy up from preschool
- Go to play date, playground, class, library
- Run last minute errands for dinner, get car washed, etc.
- Make dinner
- Bathe kids

- Story time
- Clean up kitchen
- Check e-mails, voice mail, return correspondence, process orders, fold laundry, make shopping list

Albert's list was a little shorter:

- Feed dogs
- Take dogs out for their walk
- Go to chiropractor
- Go to work: nonstop meetings, phone calls, attending to clients and employees
- Spend quality time with kids
- Feed dogs and take them for their walk
- Sort mail and recycling

Then they needed to make a separate list of what they'd like to see get done, a list of the activities and objectives that would round out a perfect day.

Annie's ideal list:

- An hour to read up on new instruments to see who's using them to perform and teach
- Time to exercise
- Dinner with Albert
- Family time
- Catch up on filing
- Plant garden

Albert's ideal list:

- Sex
- More time with Annie

Find Creative Solutions

You may be surprised at how readily you can solve childcare disputes once you can establish who really does what. Albert knew his wife worked hard to keep things running smoothly, but he had no idea that there was literally no time in her day to relax for a few minutes. Annie was touched to see that in his mind he was carving out quality time for the boys, and that he wished he could do the same with his wife. They combined their lists and ranked each activity in the order of importance, finding new ways to organize their time. Albert, who was a bit of a neat freak, agreed to take on several chores that didn't take a lot of time or that could be done at his convenience, such as the garbage detail and vacuuming the floors once a week.

He also came up with another idea to free up Annie's schedule. Annie only cooked out of necessity, not because she loved to, so he suggested signing up for a meal delivery service twice a week, and he brought home prepared dishes from the supermarket across from his office on the other days. Being responsible for the boys' dinner would also ensure that he got home in time to eat with the family. In addition, he made one other suggestion: they didn't need the money Annie earned through her job with the guitar store; it was just a job that made her feel like she was using her brain. What if she quit and instead started offering music lessons at the house? At first she could just have one or two students while the baby attended a local Mother's Day Out program, but as the kids got older and were away from home more, she could expand her student roster.

Show Need

Sometimes we do our jobs a little too well. You may believe your spouse should know how much you do, but sometimes you simply have to be more specific and vocal about how much you are doing and where you need help. Annie thought she had been very clear about how overloaded and unhappy she was, but she was so good at keeping everything running smoothly that Albert couldn't begin to comprehend how hard it really was. You have to remember to show your need.

Give and Give

You will be delighted at how fluidly the positive feelings you get following a mutually beneficial renegotiation of one aspect of your life spill over into other aspects. When a mom believes that her spouse is helping her feel better about mothering, for example, she usually starts to feel better about her role as a wife and lover as well.

Over time, as she enjoyed how Albert's solutions altered the frantic rhythm of her days and she felt less like she had run a marathon by the time the kids were in bed, Annie's interactions with her husband grew warmer. She made a more conscious effort to cuddle with him on the couch after the kids were in bed and to accept his sexual overtures. She started surprising him by showing him the pretty lingerie she'd buy to wear under the nice clothes she wore on their semimonthly outings. By the end of the evening, neither of them could wait to get them off.

Annie and Albert did not negotiate a purely fair deal. Annie did not get her primary wish, which was to see Albert take on more childcare. But the process opened her eyes to what Albert provided her and her family, and helped her appreciate everything he did do. Learning to accept someone the way he is a tremendously important skill. Once Annie was able to allow Albert's weaknesses and acknowledge his strengths, she was able to let go of her resentment and appreciate him for who he was. And, as a testament to how things can change if you just hang on for the long haul, her patience was rewarded once the boys got older and she saw her husband blossom into the comfortable and hands-on father she had known he could be.

Adolescence

You'd think that by the time children reach adolescence, their parents would have gotten their parenting styles in sync and would be well prepared to take on the challenge. But raising a person through puberty is a whole new ballgame. The problems are bigger, the emotions are more volatile, and the homework is harder. Many parents feel like they're in a perpetual state of anxiety as they imagine all the ways their teenagers' hormones, impulsivity, and lack of intellectual override can get them into trouble as they get into cars, start deciding whether to have sex or try drugs, and experiment with different identities. All of that anxiety is infectious and can seep into your interactions with your spouse, putting a strain on your marriage.

> ### Put Worrying on Hold
>
> One way to get through this stage is to try not to worry about your teenager ahead of time, especially regarding those situations you cannot control. Anticipating the worst before it happens is a waste of psychic energy that would be used more effectively if it were focused on finding ways to keep you and your spouse bonded, and laughing, through this challenging period.

One common source of friction between couples as their teens stretch their wings is the discovery that each parent has a different idea of what boundaries are appropriate. Do any of these sound familiar?

- "Jeanne, this isn't the Victorian era. If you keep being so strict with Andrew you're just going to push him away."
- "For Pete's sake, Harold, you're supposed to be his father, not his friend. You always take his side. I don't like hearing him call girls 'hotties.'"

- "Tell me I did not just hear you give Shannon permission to go on a date? She's only fourteen. I don't want her riding around in a car with a boy. I was a boy, I know what can happen."

If these differences of opinion sound all too familiar, it's time to take another look at the implicit parenting agreement you forged back when you first started having children. With a little renegotiation, you and your spouse can put up a stronger united front as your adolescent children do their very best to turn your hair prematurely white.

Aviva and Jon

Before they had kids, Aviva and Jon would have long conversations about how they planned to raise them. Aviva had been limited to an hour a day of television when she was a child, and she thought that was a good rule to live by. In addition, she believed that summers were a time when kids, and especially teenagers, should be developing themselves or engaging in constructive, stimulating activities or jobs that would look good on college applications. Jon spent entire summers watching cartoons or playing video games when he was growing up and still managed to get into college and get a good job, but he agreed that less TV is probably better for kids.

When their kids were thirteen and fifteen, Aviva still tried to limit the television watching when she was home. Jon, who was home more often, completely ignored the one-hour-of-TV-a-day rule. When Aviva tried to make the children turn it off, she was ignored. Turning to Jon for support, he usually mumbled a halfhearted, "Kids, listen to your mother," but there were no consequences when they did not. Aviva simmered with resentment under an otherwise placid surface, and didn't see why she should give Jon sex when he wouldn't give her the support she needed to raise her children right.

Renegotiating How You Support Each Other While Parenting

Aviva knew that if she didn't help Jon understand how angry and hurt she was, their marriage was going to be in serious trouble. One day, during a moment of unaccustomed calm over the breakfast table, she presented Jon with a list of all the rules and standards she thought the kids should follow and aspire to. Then she explained why the list mattered to her.

"We need to push them to do and be more while we still have some influence. Sadie is so interested in science, we should be seeing what kind of summer internships are available to teenagers at the medical center. And Billy should be playing basketball, not pretending to play it on the Wii. But it's gotten to the point where the kids just tune me out because they know that when Mom talks, no one has to listen. If you spoke up, they'd start to pay attention. I need you to back me up. If I were a single mother I'd be prepared to do this alone, but you're supposed to be my partner. I want our kids to see us do this together."

Jon was taken aback. Aviva had never sounded so vulnerable. Through the process of writing her list, Aviva had figured out how to express her feelings of impotence as well as her dreams for the children. Jon began to realize that unintentionally he was sabotaging the goals for all of the people he loved. Jon began to open his mind to new possibilities. He was talented in creating presentations for his freelance marketing business; why not use his skills where they were just as important?

"You're right. I need to help more. Hey, I have an idea."

When the kids got back from the pool that afternoon, they found that their father had put up a big bulletin board with the heading, "Our Family Rules," listing most of the rules Aviva had outlined on her list, including a few he had asked to modify. He had also downloaded information on a number of teen-oriented programs and announced that after dinner they were going to sit down and figure out which ones each kid would like to apply for.

As Aviva saw Jon implement her rules over the next few weeks, and saw that they worked to give the kids a stronger sense of order and calm, just as she had hoped they would, she started to feel much warmer toward her husband, like they had joined the same winning team. Her desire to show him that warmth in bed didn't take very long to follow.

Other Ways to Stay Bonded While Raising Teens

Your teenagers will test every boundary, push every button, and rage against the injustice of your rules, but their greatest source of comfort and security will be the united front you and your partner present at every turn. Achieving that united front requires a tag team effort of complementing each other's strengths and weaknesses, which means you have to keep talking (and talking, and talking) so that you're aware of what those strengths and weaknesses are, and so you know when one of you needs help. The following tips will help guide your conversations.

Remember Your Youth

Share memories with your partner about what it was like when you were a teenager. Talk about the risks you took, and explain why you do or don't regret them. Try to see what you might have been like through your parents' eyes. By sharing these memories, you're giving each other fuel to use when one of you needs a reminder to stay compassionate with your teen, even if you're ready to throttle him or her.

Renegotiate Your Perspective

Agree to do whatever you can to keep your perspective (remember that the long view is more important than the short-term), and to ask for help when you feel like you can't. If you see your spouse starting to get bogged down with worry, bring up one of those stories you shared about the ridiculous things you did as a teen, and remind her that you made it through okay and so will your child.

Renegotiate What's Funny

Help each other keep a sense of humor. If you see your husband begin to seethe when the music gets so loud the walls start to shake, dance around to the music and make him laugh before allowing him to go upstairs to ask your daughter to turn the volume down. This strategy changes your partner's brain chemistry from fight or flight to mellow and calm.

Renegotiate What's Cool

If you can't fight 'em, join 'em. Teens can keep you youthful if you're willing to give them a chance. When you're in the car together, ask your teen to let everyone hear the music he's got on his iPod, and ask him why he likes it so much. Show him that you take his tastes seriously and that you're interested in branching out your own.

Young Adulthood

For some parents, watching children leave home to start their own lives is liberating, and for others it's heartbreak. It's a major renegotiation moment as they rewrite the contract they had with their child and spouse that identified their role as parent. It is always a time when couples are forced to turn to each other and ask, "Now what?"

The couples who are best prepared to weather the transition to the empty nest are the ones who all along negotiated their way through the other phases in their children's lives. At each stage, they took stock in where they were emotionally, checked in to make sure they were ready to support each other's parenting decisions, and worked to keep their life as a twosome going strong. They made sure to have a lot going on in their lives other than the kids, even as they involved themselves deeply in their children's existence. The bittersweet feeling of watching your chick fly away can be tempered if you can then turn to your spouse and say with a smile, "I am so excited to start the rest of my life with you."

If you find yourself facing an empty nest, and realize that you feel disconnected from your spouse, now is the perfect opportunity to renegotiate all the parameters of your relationship and make sure you are both getting exactly what you need.

Negotiating Your New Life

Now that you're free of the obligations of day-to-day parenting, it's time for a little "good narcissism," which means taking a healthy approach to self-fulfillment and developing self-love. As you'll see in the chapter about hobbies, focusing on yourself can be a fantastic way to rekindling the fire in your marriage that might have gotten a little smothered by the responsibilities of parenthood.

1. Talk out your feelings.

Find a time when you can have a calm, honest conversation with your spouse about your feelings. "Now that the kids are gone, I'm feeling a little lonely. I think having them around made it easy for us to ignore the fact that we've gotten a little distant from each other. I've signed up for that photography class I've always talked about. Would you want to take it with me? You've got such a natural eye."

2. Court each other.

Start dating again. Imagine what you would do if you were taking your spouse on a first date. How would you dress? What would you plan? Then do it.

3. Rekindle desire.

Now that you don't have to spend time on the kids, start spending more time on yourself. Get involved in all the activities you've never had time for. Take the classes that didn't used to fit into your schedule because you had to leave room for the kids' activities. As you further develop your interests and passions, you'll see a new sparkle in your spouse's eye.

4. Be compassionate.

It's rare that both parents will react exactly the same to a newly child-free house. One might need to mourn the loss, and the other might be ecstatic with her new freedom. That person has to do her best to show compassion to the person who is struggling. With compassion, she will also help her spouse recognize that she can help provide the connection he feels he has lost.

5. Understand intent.

As a couple gets used to the new dilemmas brought about by adult children—will they come home for the holidays, will they bring someone with them, what if they don't want to come home?—understanding each other's intent will help you avoid judging your partner for not feeling the same way you do. For example, you think the perfect vacation involves renting a big house on the beach and inviting all the kids and grandkids to join you there for a month. When your plans are met with less than enthusiasm, don't assume that it's because your partner doesn't love family and the children as much as you do. In fact, don't ever assume anything. Ask. Talk. Negotiate.

How to Ask, Talk, and Negotiate ────────────

Here's a sample conversation that shows how two partners can negotiate without assumptions.

"I can't imagine anything nicer than being with the kids over the holidays. Don't you miss them?"

"Of course I do. But you and I haven't had a vacation together, just the two of us, in thirty years. I'd rather take all the money we'd spend on a big family month together and invest it on a short retreat to somewhere exotic, just the two of us. Imagine, no interruptions, no schedule but our own, no having to check in on where the kids are or when they're coming back. It'll be heaven."

"Mmm, that does sound delightful. Well, what about a compromise? Could we coordinate a week on the beach with the kids and devote the rest of our time to being alone together?"

"It's going to be hard to get everyone in one place for just one week. No one's schedule ever seems to match up."

"True. I promise not to let my nose get bent out of shape if not everyone can make the date we choose. Those who can come will come, and those who can't, well, we'll talk to them first the next time we set up a family holiday. How does that sound?"

"Perfect."

Homeward Bound

No matter how much you love your children, and no matter how sad you were to let them go when it was time, watching them move back in with you can be extremely difficult. Whether they need to come home because a rough economic climate has made it impossible for them to find a job, or because of illness or a breakup, allowing your adult child to live with you again requires real negotiating skills to make sure that your life as a couple isn't frayed.

Create a Contract with Your Spouse

When making the decision of whether or when to allow your child to move back in, make sure to put down in writing all of your concerns, and lay out a strategy for handling every one. Even if you are sure that the arrangement will be short lived, agree on preset times when you and your spouse will get together to talk privately about what is and isn't working, and what you plan to do about it.

Create a Contract with Your Child

Have your child sign a contract promising to uphold whatever rules or agreements he or she has agreed to in exchange for moving back in. That way no one can claim ignorance.

Protect Your Time

Do not allow the presence of your child to infringe on the time you have built as a couple. Sacrifices needed to be made when your children were young. Now, though, it is the child who needs to make the sacrifice. By taking him or her in you are providing support in a time of need. That doesn't mean that you must revert back to the roles you graduated from years ago.

Children grow up and become independent, but once they're gone, a couple only has each other. When you remember to balance the needs of your marriage with those of your children—and occasionally be willing to put your marriage ahead of your children—you stand a far better chance of staying together for a lifetime.

Chapter 7

Money: Balancing Your Power Along with Your Budget

Seventy-six percent of Americans named money as the number one source of stress in their lives, according to a 2011 American Psychological Association survey. In addition, money is the number one topic of disagreement in young marriages. As much as sex, desire, health issues, kids, in-laws, jobs, religion, and any number of other topics can be a lightning rod between couples, nothing comes close to causing the kind of flaming, explosive fights as often as money does.

Of all the topics we have covered so far, money is the most arduous to negotiate, because the shame and taboo it evokes make people reluctant to even bring it up. But you can't negotiate through anything if you're not willing to face the underlying cause of your disagreement. You can't bargain for an improved sex life if the reason your wife is withholding sex is that she believes you're hiding something because you won't give her the online passwords to the bank accounts. You can't achieve trust if you feel infantilized when every time you ask your wife, the main breadwinner of the family, how much you have in savings, she simply replies, "Enough."

Couples who are in this predicament often assume that if they ever start to talk about finances, they would find that their differences are irreconcilable. Actually, most people aren't that far apart in their philosophy. Talking about money is difficult; finding solutions to money conflicts is frequently easier than predicted.

Removing the Taboo

We are a conflicted lot when it comes to money discussions. In a 2011 Lawyers.com "Couples and Money" survey of over 1,000 adults in committed relationships, 91 percent said that they believe it's important to discuss each other's financial histories before getting married, yet over a quarter admitted to avoiding the topic altogether. And though 40 percent of people said they believed that it is more important to be honest about money than it is to be about your sexual history or your fidelity, nearly 29 percent said they withheld information from their spouse about their discretionary spending habits.

Why? Because many people believe that thinking or talking about money makes them look greedy. Speaking about sex might be uncomfortable, but the underlying goal of the discussion is usually to bring you closer to your spouse, to enhance your pleasure and intimacy together. Many people think talking about money just makes them look avaricious, materialistic, or superficial. No one wants to seem that way.

Who Is at Risk

Money equals security and power, and you have neither if you feel anxious because you don't know how much you and your spouse really have, or resentful because you can't get your partner to stick to a budget, or angry because you feel you should be earning more than he is by now. People lash out when they feel vulnerable. Money factors into so many decisions couples make—where to live, where to shop, what to eat, whether to have children, whether to vacation, and on and on—it's no wonder it's the source of so much friction in the majority of households.

Yet there are two family dynamics that are particularly vulnerable to cash conflicts: in households where one spouse doesn't work, or in families where the wife earns more than the husband. Sometimes if a woman is dating a man who earns less than she does, she won't bring up the subject for fear of humiliating and ultimately losing him. There's no reason for those feelings to dissipate once she marries him. A man might not want to be honest about how much he makes for fear that he won't find a woman who will love him for who he is but rather for how much he is worth, or that the woman he marries will spend it all if she finds out how much there really is in the bank.

If you are in these kinds of relationships, even if you are confident that finances is not causing an undertow in your marriage, take a moment to consider bringing up the subject with your spouse or even taking a renegotiating step or two. You might be surprised to find that you or your partner is unknowingly carrying some residually negative feelings about your arrangement. Better to smooth them out now than to wait for them to fester and explode.

Negotiating 101

When renegotiating money in a marriage, what you're really bargaining for is a balance in power. In many cases, negotiating money merely requires a commitment to sharing information and increased transparency. That's usually all it takes for partners to feel more secure and to ease tensions. The reality is rarely as terrifying as the scenarios we weave in our imaginations.

Bob and Carol

When Bob and Carol first met, Carol was a music teacher. They married and enjoyed a couple of fun, bohemian years. Eventually, however, they recognized that if they wanted to have children they were going to need to make more money. "I'll die if you stick me in a nine-to-five job with a boss breathing down my back, though," swore Bob. So Carol, who already had a business degree, went back to school, got her master's, and quickly found work at an investment firm. She was happy that her high, steady income allowed Bob to continue building his independent music production company. She'd just live her artistic fantasies vicariously through him, she thought. They moved out of the city, had a son, got a dog, and adopted a typical suburban life.

Carol was extremely good at her job but Bob had chosen a career in a field where it was proving exceedingly hard for most big companies to make any money, much less a small independent producer. Bob believed that his business would be viable if people would quit cheating him. The fact that he continued to show impulsive, poor judgment and had made some big mistakes rarely factored into his view of himself as a victim. Carol was glad she could pay off his debt the first time, feeling that she was supporting Bob's dream, but when she had to do it a second time and Bob still refused to consider changing careers, or even changing his business model, she started to feel used.

As Bob's debt grew, his mood became increasingly foul at home. Carol, tired of the negativity and progressively more convinced that he would never be solvent, began to retreat into her work and her child. Though once they had enjoyed heading into the city to hear new bands together, they rarely went out anymore, and their sex life had become nonexistent.

The day that Bob finally admitted that he was going to need to dip into the family's savings again to cover his business debts,

Carol let loose a cascade of venom that even she wasn't aware she had been holding back. And Bob fought back just as hard.

In many cases, when years of resentment and anger finally break the surface, ugly exchanges like these can be the death knell for a marriage. That's unfortunate, because it's often only in moments like these, when both partners are finally exposing their darkest thoughts and feelings, that the renegotiation can begin.

Three Steps to Renegotiating Your Financial Life

Having honest conversations about money can be hard and make you feel extremely vulnerable. Don't let your feelings get translated into aggression or defensiveness. Keeping the conversation calm, focused, and task-oriented will help you get through the initial awkwardness until you come up with a solution that feels right for you both. Once you're there, you'll find that the conversation, if it needs to happen again, will be easier each time. These three steps will help keep your discussion on track:

Speak Calmly

The feelings people express during big fights need to be aired, but no one can really hear the other when the message is delivered cruelly and angrily. Fortunately, after their blowout, Bob and Carol took a few days apart to calm down and gather their thoughts. As they considered their options, their view of their son, and what would happen to him if they couldn't reconcile, compelled them to come back together and try to work things out.

The next time they talked, Bob and Carol discussed how to move forward, and said how they felt, but in a calmer, more con- structive way. Carol reaffirmed how much she appreciated and supported Bob's artistry, but said that for many years the family money had gone to support a business that just wasn't working.

Bob explained that he felt the losses were not really his fault—he did his best, but as soon as his artists had any success, they went on to bigger companies. And Carol expressed that this was probably the nature of the business, and offered a compromise: she could continue to support him financially and emotionally if he would be less volatile around the house. That, she felt, would make a difference in their relationship. Once Bob realized how emotionally stressful the situation was for Carol, he was able to agree to make some changes.

Give and Give

When we bear witness to our partner's attempts to work on the relationship, we're usually compelled to increase our efforts, as well. Kindness can beget kindness. Compromise often begets compromise. As he learned just how stressful their arrangement had become for Carol, Bob began to try to think more openly and creatively about how he could continue to work within the industry that he loved but make more income. He realized he needed to become less rigid in his judgment about what was truly "selling out"—something he simply couldn't bear doing.

For example, he finally agreed to start renting out his studio space, which Carol had begged him to do from the very beginning. And when a friend of his suggested that there was a job that would be perfect for him at the children's cable channel where he worked, Bob controlled his knee-jerk reaction to dismiss it as sell-out work and agreed to come in for an interview.

As Bob started to give Carol a more open, positive, and responsible attitude, Carol was compelled to give him more of herself. She was greatly moved that Bob would consider closing the business in the interest of making her happy. By showing Carol his willingness to reconsider positions he'd previously said were unthinkable, and by softening his cynicism, he gave Carol a lot more incentive to find a way to help him keep his business afloat. Buoyed by the new sense of being on the same team, the tension in the house started to ease up, and their lovemaking increased.

Get Into the Details

You can do a lot to ease money's grip on your relationship by bluntly discussing your financial philosophy and goals even before marriage. But it's never too late. When was the last time you and your spouse had a heart-to-heart, not just about the money that's in the bank, but about your financial philosophy?

What does money mean to you? Are you a spender or a saver? Do you prefer to use money on tangible things or on experiences? Employ these conversations as a springboard into a more specific discussion about your personal finances. What can we afford, how much do we have to save, what are our long-term and short-term financial goals?

Also, discuss what economic obligations you each brought to the marriage, such as student debt, alimony, child support, or elderly parents. Have those obligations changed? If so, a renegotiation is in order. Ultimately, the secret to protecting your marriage from fiscal stress is transparency.

Though many people would harshly judge someone for staying in a marriage because they enjoy the material comforts it provides, it's not the worst reason to stay in a marriage. If there are kids, it's a very good reason. The children shouldn't have to experience a decline in their living arrangements just because their parents can't figure out how to rethink their expectations of each other. But there's a bigger reason. In general, if you stick out a marriage, most people come back around and realize that they do love their spouse, and they learn to appreciate them more. Tenacity is a big factor in the longevity of a marriage.

Chapter 8

Career Transitions: Following Your Dream Without Leaving Anyone Behind

It's difficult to keep our lives compartmentalized—what influences one area of our existence generally bleeds into other parts as well. That's why it's not surprising that studies show a strong link between job satisfaction and matrimonial harmony. If you hate your job, there's a good chance your relationship with your spouse is suffering, too, and the more conflict that exists within your family, the less satisfied you probably are with your job. The research also shows that the opposite is true: the more you like your job, the less conflict probably exists within your family.

The good news is that aside from periods of economic instability, historically ours is a society that encourages and facilitates professional mobility, so if we find ourselves miserable in a job or career, with enough chutzpah, ingenuity, and determination, we can often make a change for the better. It's a triumph when we take control of our career and turn it in the direction we wish it to go, or even abandon it altogether in favor of something that will be far more challenging or fulfilling. The bad news is that often the professional changes that benefit us aren't always quite so beneficial to our spouse, at least in the short term.

Interestingly, as reported by Johanna Peetz and Lara Kammrath in a May 2011 issue of the *Journal of Personality and Social Psychology*, the couples that are the most effusive in the courting days of their relationships are also usually the ones that have the greatest difficulty navigating a spouse's career transition. The reason is that these infatuated, gushing, demonstrative couples are more prone to making huge, sweeping promises to each other than their more reserved, rational counterparts. But these kinds of promises are also extremely hard to keep.

Even if we know realistically that our mate's ambitions might be a little pie-in-the-sky, our affection makes it easy for us to be swept up in our lover's exuberance. By the time reality hits and our spouse realizes that, say, she isn't going to have her own design label by her thirtieth birthday, our hormones have died down a bit and we might feel a little disappointed that the person we chose as our mate isn't going to be the superstar we assumed she'd be.

Though theoretically most of us know that when we get married we will sometimes be asked to make compromises, we rarely anticipate just how dramatically some of those compromises will affect us. A stay-at-home mom can be proud and delighted when her husband makes partner and still be unhappy that it also results in his spending even more hours at the office and away from the family. You may see your wife's transfer to a different division in Taiwan as the chance to take an adventure and still be terrified to give up your job and move to a country where your skill set isn't much in demand.

At junctures like these, it is imperative that partners reexamine the assumptions and expectations they've harbored about their careers. Generally, a couple will benefit by taking small, realistic steps toward renegotiating life after a major career change. As you see the positive effects of these steps on your relationship, the bigger alterations resulting from the career change will seem far less overwhelming.

Martha and Eugene

Taking little steps is how Martha weathered the major change in her life when her orthopedist husband, Eugene, announced that he wanted to get out of private practice and instead travel the world with Doctors Without Borders.

At first Martha felt betrayed. She loved the idea of being a doctor's wife, and had been proud to marry someone who could heal others and make a great living doing it. Eugene reminded her of her father, whom she adored and admired, a quiet, shy man who had nonetheless run a successful general practice in their rural Ohio town.

But since their wedding day, it had been hard for Eugene to build a viable private practice in their mid-sized city. He was indeed like Martha's father, quiet and shy—too shy to network and make friends with the referring doctors at the hospital where he had privileges. Being the only general practitioner for several miles had meant that Martha's father had never had to seek out patients, but Eugene, practicing in a far more competitive environment, was struggling to stay busy. Martha thought she would have the option of staying home with the children just as her mother had, but in the end their finances required that she keep her job as an office manager.

Though a little disappointed that her husband hadn't reached the professional heights she had envisioned, she was generally happy with their life together and thought he was, too, though she had noticed that he could be morose, and was spending too much time alone in front of the TV.

She didn't realize how long it had been since she had seen him get genuinely excited about something until the day he came to her and announced that he wanted to join Doctors Without Borders.

Martha's initial reaction was explosive. In the weeks that followed, they hardly spoke to each other. Martha was outraged at the unfair sacrifice she believed Eugene had asked her to make.

She imagined how hard it would be to raise the kids alone, and worried about what would happen to Eugene if he wound up in a disease-ridden, war-torn country. Soon, though, she could see that the children were starting to react to the tension in the house and that somehow they were going to have to resolve this conflict.

Five Steps to Renegotiating a Career Transition

Springing the news of a career change on your unsuspecting spouse requires finesse. Before saying anything, consider how your partner generally reacts to the unexpected. Does he get excited, does he yell with fear, does he withdraw? Keeping your spouse's feelings in mind will help you come up with a gentle, unthreatening way to break your news, and avoid getting angry or defensive if the reaction isn't what you had hoped. The following steps will help you make sure your spouse feels safe when he or she hears what could be life-changing news.

Get Away

Whenever possible, take your negotiation to neutral territory away from any distractions or stressors.

Martha and Eugene decided to take a week's vacation together so they could have plenty of time to talk about the big change Eugene was proposing. The first day there, they didn't try to tackle the subject, preferring to simply enjoy the gorgeous surroundings and spend time swimming and relaxing. The next day, though, after breakfast, Martha took a deep breath.

"Ok. Tell me why you want to join Doctors Without Borders." She tried to stay as calm and nonjudgmental as possible, and told herself not to react to anything he said, just to listen.

With this simple question she gave Eugene the chance to explain how deeply miserable he had been at work, and how the research he had done into the Doctors Without Borders organization had convinced him that working with that organization is where he could do the most good for people. He was sure that he could continue to earn a steady income that wouldn't require any move or material sacrifice from Martha or the children. As he spoke about the good he imagined he could accomplish, Martha started to see glimmers of the passionate, inspired man with whom she had fallen in love. He was asking her to renegotiate their contract so that he could uphold the one he had made with himself about being a healer. She knew she could not refuse.

But she couldn't just let him go off across the world without making sure that her needs were going to be met, too. She couldn't face an insecure future. The rest of the week was spent brainstorming specific, practical ideas to negotiate how Eugene would stay connected to the family from far away, and how he and Martha would keep their relationship strong.

Create Rituals

A career transition can upend an entire family, but negotiating rituals as you adjust can offer everyone a great deal of comfort in the midst of change. Martha had often tried to initiate small family rituals, such as family game night, but these had fallen by the wayside as the kids had grown older. Now she insisted on creating new ones. She and Eugene negotiated that every evening at 10 P.M. he would Skype the family. The children could each choose to speak to him privately for ten minutes and then Martha and Eugene would spend the rest of the time having their own conversation.

Make Your Partner the Priority

Whoever is instigating the career change needs to make sure that his or her partner doesn't feel overshadowed in the midst of all the excitement. Eugene needed to make Martha feel like she's the most important person in his life—more important than his patients. They agreed to set up a special number that Martha could use to call Eugene before 10 P.M., almost as if she were an emergency patient. This way Martha knew that she could always have access to Eugene in a way that no one else could. She had VIP status.

Plan Special Time Together

Carving out face-to-face time is imperative when people are adjusting to change. Eugene committed to coming home for a week every five weeks, and the family had to be able to visit him for a week at a time whenever there was a school vacation. If he was stationed in a dangerous area, they would arrange to meet midway in a European country. Finally, Eugene and Martha agreed to spend three long weekends alone together each year, no excuses.

Before they left their negotiation getaway, the calendar was filled out for the coming year. That weekend the couple made love more often than they had since the children were born. Eugene was nervous about his upcoming adventure but ecstatic that he had his wife's support, and Martha was intrigued to find out what this new chapter in their lives would look like.

Though soon they would spend less time in each other's presence than they had since they met, the effort they put into sustaining their relationship, and especially their sense of intimacy, actually improved and strengthened their marriage.

Take Your Time

Sometimes negotiating through a major reorientation such as a career shift that requires a change in lifestyle needs to take place over a longer stretch of time than a weekend or even a week. If you implement modification in small doses and give yourself time to adjust, couples often discover that the anticipation of change is far more stressful or difficult to get used to than the actual change itself.

When Career Transitions Transform Your Power Dynamics

Career shifts aren't a challenge only because they require so much adjustment from one's spouse, but also because they can force the couple to alter any unspoken fiscal contracts they made that have governed their spending, saving, and influence dynamics. This can often arise when a spouse decides to leave a high-powered, lucrative position in favor of something more fulfilling or service-oriented, such as a nonprofit or a teaching position. But believe it or not, reinventing yourself in a financially upward direction can cause just as much of a rift in your relationship as taking a pay cut.

All negotiations, whether personal or business, are ultimately about balancing control, and the imbalance of clout and lack of a decision-making process can do harm in any marriage.

Debbie and John

Debbie was floored when John announced out of the blue that he had accepted a position as a trader on Wall Street. He had neither told her he was thinking of leaving his job as a social worker, nor that he had gotten an interview with a big firm through a friend whose trading group was looking for a smart, cheap, entry-level replacement. The friend knew that John was a strong numbers guy, and when he heard that John was mulling over a career switch, he had been happy to open a few doors for him.

Before renegotiating, John first had to admit the assumptions and behaviors that had led to his belief that the only way to negotiate his career change was behind Debbie's back.

Early on, they had developed an implicit marriage contract of domination and submission. To avoid conflict with Debbie, John would do things on the sly. What she didn't know wouldn't hurt her, he figured. But what John did not realize is that by avoiding direct confrontation he was in effect manipulating Debbie.

He also never imagined that his decision to change careers would actually put his marriage at risk. He knew Debbie would be upset with him for his secretiveness, but he assumed that when she realized how much easier it would be for them to keep up with her wealthy friends, and how much he was looking forward to spoiling her more, she'd get over it. He hadn't really absorbed that his original career choice was one of the reasons Debbie had married him.

Debbie had chafed under the way her parents dangled rewards in front of her and then withdrew them when she didn't perform to their expectations. She resented how they had used money to control her, keeping her on a tight budgetary leash and refusing to help pay her way to her first choice university. She didn't experience her initial real taste of freedom until she got her first job, and after that she swore she would never be financially dependent again.

When she met John at a singles event and found out that he was working at a welfare office in the Bronx, she practically fell in love on the spot. She had married the man of her dreams, one who was idealistic, kind, handsome, and not interested in making more money than she made. With John, she thought she would always be in control of her destiny.

But as John flourished in his new position and began to make significant trades and generous commissions, Debbie began to question her future with him. Her sense of safety was so threatened she would make up any reason not to come home, choosing instead to put in increasingly long hours at the office. Not only had the money balance shifted, but John's fear of confrontation made Debbie mistrustful of what else he was not telling her.

Understanding Your Past Arrangement

When a career shift alters the power dynamics of your relationship, you must renegotiate so that you both understand the benefits and weakness of your past arrangement. Only then will you be able to get excited about the future reward of your new beginning. This discussion will allow each person in the couple to feel as if control is being shared instead of usurped. As you discuss how you want your financial life to look, pay special attention to:

1. The routines that have worked in the past.
2. How envy, jealousy, and fear of being left behind could affect the partner whose career is not shifting.
3. Making a plan to negotiate a time when the partner who is currently in the status quo gets a chance to discuss his dreams for a new beginning.

This is how John learned that Debbie was not against his making more money than she, only that she was adamant about not being controlled by his money. It is also how they figured out that Debbie wanted John to stand up to her, so that she no longer had to worry that he was sneaking around behind her back to get what he wanted.

Once those fundamentals had been established, they were able to negotiate into which accounts their earnings would go, what could be reserved for fixed expenses, and what would be invested. In this way, they achieved a comfortable and balanced sense of personal and financial control over their relationship. Now Debbie no longer felt threatened by John's career shift, and also John knew that he must be forthright with her going forward, as avoiding his discomfort with Debbie's disapproval only led to a worse reaction, Debbie's distrust.

Create a Decision-Making Plan ─────────────

As early as possible in your marriage, create a decision-making plan that allows each partner to have his or her fair share of input whenever you come to a crossroads. Periodically schedule a time to do the following things:

1. Hold a state of the union meeting, maybe every six months, to evaluate whether anything has changed and whether your mutual goals have shifted.
2. Indulge in some blue-sky dreams about what you'd like to do next.

Negotiating Your Career Needs Along with Those of Your Spouse

When a career transition seems to benefit one spouse overwhelmingly more than the other, the spouse with dreams of changing careers needs to tap into serious empathy to make sure the other partner feels like her professional satisfaction matters, too.

Adjusting to change can make life exciting, unpredictable, and better than we could ever have imagined it to be. For a flourishing marriage allow your spouse to have influence and participation in any changes you want to instigate.

Chapter 9

Job Loss: Embracing Who You Are Instead of What You Do

How many times have you met someone new and the first thing they ask is, "And what do you do?" How many times have you asked this question yourself? As much as we profess that we value people for who they are and not how much they earn or what circles they run in, the fact that so many conversations begin with inquiries into what we do for a living indicates that our identities are extremely wrapped up in the subject.

It's no wonder, then, that a job loss can cut to the core of a person's sense of self, and wreak havoc on their feeling of stability, well-being, and confidence. For those who truly identify with their work, a job loss can be a cruel blow to self-respect and one's experience of fulfillment. Even if you're extremely self-aware you might find it hard to focus on shoring up those intangibles when you're stressed about finances. Yet you must, because once you recognize that it was the sense of accomplishment you got from your job that fulfilled you, and not the job itself, you'll realize that you can recreate that emotion anywhere.

Principles of Renegotiating Through a Job Loss

It's no fun being out of work; there aren't a lot of happy feelings associated with it. Even if you happen to have loathed your job and got such a massive severance you don't have to worry about money, it's almost impossible for a job loss to leave a person emotionally unscathed. Couples who successfully renegotiate through a job loss tap into something that not everyone has in abundance: a sense of well-being. Psychologist Martin Seligman identifies five elements to well-being in his book, *Flourish*:

1. Positive Emotion—When you approach your life with a glass half-full attitude, you're better prepared to negotiate with yourself whenever something happens that you did not plan. You're also able to instill confidence in anyone who is affected by your job loss, especially your life partner.
2. Relationships—A person who allows his spouse to offer comfort, help, and support as he explores new possibilities will be better able to handle the process with patience and equanimity.
3. Engagement—This refers to how you feel when you're focused on or entranced by what you're doing so that you don't even notice the time pass. It's also been called "flow." Some people who are out of work may worry they'll never experience this feeling again. But those who are determined will find a new passion to engage in "flow" once again. For some it could be soccer, for others it might be pottery or photography, for still others it is becoming a triathlete. The possibilities are endless. Search for it and you will find it.
4. Meaning—Truly positive people find meaning in everything they do. A teacher turned taxi driver does not necessarily find his life less fulfilling so long as he keeps an open mind and looks for meaning where he can find it. Couples who live according

to these principles are well prepared to negotiate through the challenges a job loss can present.

5. Accomplishments—People experience a sense of accomplishment in ways from major to mundane. Finishing a marathon would definitely give someone a sense of accomplishment, but so can planting your flowerbeds or cleaning off your desk.

Job loss is a drag but it can often give you a gift of free time to pursue avenues you've never tried before. Maybe in between sending out resumes and making phone calls you coach a hockey team or tutor a fifth grader. Finding ways to continue feeling accomplished and productive allows you to remain the connected partner your spouse still needs.

Many families see their relationships fray when the strain of a job loss starts to infiltrate their everyday existence. Everyone feels like a contract has been broken. Until you accept that a new one must be renegotiated to accommodate the changed circumstances, no one will be able to move forward and see alternative opportunities that are inevitably around the corner. To get there, you must reconnect with your sense of well-being by seeking to reinstill Seligman's five elements into your life.

Ron and Barb

When the music publishing company Ron worked for closed, at first he didn't take it too hard. Ron's wife, Barb, a lawyer, earned enough to keep the family afloat, and at first Ron didn't mind playing Mr. Mom to their two children, Barry and Elle. It was the first time that he had really gotten to listen to twelve-year-old Barry's band rehearse in the garage, and he enjoyed hanging out with them and giving them pointers. He was also flattered at how his ten-year-old daughter, Elle, beamed with pride when she could see her father watching her with all the mothers during her hip-hop class.

None of her friends had ever had as much time with their dads as she was getting. But as the weeks of unemployment turned to months, and then the year anniversary of his layoff came and went, Ron's mood soured and he began to get angry and bitter.

He started to feel humiliated that he couldn't provide the lifestyle his family had previously enjoyed. Barb's salary was just enough to put food on the table, pay the mortgage, and fill up the car. All the extras—the restaurant dinners, the movies, the weekend trips, the perks that permitted them to keep up with their neighbors—were no longer possible. They had to let go of the housekeeper who came every two weeks, and with Ron's negligible housekeeping skills the home began to feel cluttered and chaotic. The kids didn't understand why their parents were suddenly so stingy, whereas before they'd get passed an extra twenty dollars or so to spend on an outing with their friends. As time went on, the kids got snippy and disrespectful as they absorbed the implication of what their reduced family finances would mean for them. Barb started to wilt under the stress of carrying the family's fiscal welfare on her back, and Ron sank further and further into a sullen depression. All four members of the household were wallowing in hostility, resentment, and fear.

Negotiating Back to a Sense of Well-Being

As Barb watched her family disintegrate, she knew that something had to be done to help them all focus on what they had instead of what they didn't have. After all, they weren't destitute; they just needed to gain some perspective.

Resilient people are able to see the bright side of almost anything. Train yourself to look for the positive no matter what happens to you. Even in the mist of sadness and loss, you can find a glimmer of something for which you can be grateful.

Look for the Positive

Barb started listing as many positives as she could. She thought:

1. Good for me for being able to support a family of four.
2. The kids have never had as much time with Ron as they do now. Barry's playing has improved since Ron started listening to him practice and giving him pointers.
3. I don't actually miss those weekend trips with the Durcheks. Mindy's obsession with her diet was starting to get on my nerves anyway.
4. Now that we're not racing to all the social events and activities, we're spending more time together at home.

Subsequently Barb needed to figure out a way to convince her family to see the positive in their situation and push away the material values that were drowning them in unnecessary distress. She decided to implement a new tradition: Sunday sit-downs. Without exception, the whole family would have dinner together. Each person would get a chance to talk about the week, what had happened, what was bothering him or her. In particular, Barb insisted that they share one thing for which they were grateful, and one thing that had previously seemed important, but that they now realized was meaningless. For example, in her case, it was the membership to the upscale gym she had always enjoyed. Now she worked out at the Y, and it didn't make any difference. "Guess what? You burn the same amount of calories on a treadmill in a gym with a view of a brick wall as you do at a gym with views overlooking the park," she said. Essentially she was implementing a fixed time every week when everyone would reveal the results of the renegotiation she was asking them to have with themselves and training them to be aware of what instills a sense of fulfillment and well-being.

Appreciate Your Relationships

If the subtext to your contract is to go through life with the attitude of "we might not have much, but we still have each other" you really can't go wrong. Barb's Sunday sit-downs not only helped the family remember how much they enjoyed each other's company, but allowed them to see which relationships were important in their lives.

Ron realized his moments with his children were the highlight of his week. The kids, too, regularly mentioned how much they enjoyed spending time with their dad. They also admitted that they had learned who their true friends were. They no longer associated with acquaintances who made them feel bad about not having the spending money they once did, and had grown closer to those who didn't care or who altered their own plans to make sure they could be involved with the group's activities.

Engage

Couples who continue to look for ways to experience a sense of engagement, even in the midst of loss, are more likely to weather a crisis successfully. You can find commitment in the most mundane tasks. Ron discovered that he liked to cook, and started taking more initiative in feeding the family, which lifted a huge load off Barb when she came home at night. His coupon cutting began bordering on the obsessive, and he started competing with himself to see how he could save as much money as possible while still feeding the family healthy meals. He also took to visiting garage and estate sales, often bringing the kids along with him on the weekends.

Seek Out Meaning

Sometimes it's in the midst of loss that we are able to see what really matters. When Barb suggested moving into a smaller house so that the demands of their lives didn't surpass their resources the whole family took some time to let the idea sink in and then agreed, albeit a bit sadly, that it would be a good idea. The move offered a bonding opportunity for Ron and Barb. They enjoyed digging through the accumulated bits and bobs of so many years together, going down memory lane, and recognizing the important things—the photographs, the love letters, the inscribed books—and letting go of the detritus and space-hogging paraphernalia that ultimately didn't mean much. They got rid of more than half their stuff, saving them the expense of paying for storage while the house was on the market. The family enjoyed their house-hunting expeditions, too. The homes they looked at weren't nearly as fancy or big as the one they would leave, but they enjoyed devising home-improvement projects.

Seek Out Accomplishment

The requirement for the new house was that it have a garage that could be converted into a music/dance studio, one wall lined with drums, one wall lined with mirrors, so that the kids could practice their music and dance, and Ron had a space for his new nonprofit giving urban students a place to get some mentoring and advice on how to break into the music industry.

The Five R's ─────────────────────────────

There are five ways in which people coping with intense feelings of loss can help themselves, a microcosm of the five elements so necessary to regaining a sense of well-being:

1. Rethink—Create a positive story out of your defeating situation.
2. Reduce—Slow life down and learn how to play again.
3. Relax—Appreciate your surroundings and pamper yourself.
4. Release—Stop worrying, start exercising, keep laughing.
5. Reorganize—Become more flexible and focus on one small step at a time.

A New Beginning

Change is a lot less frightening or upsetting when we can see how a new beginning will give us opportunities to achieve things we hadn't imagined before. In the end, Ron's job loss brought this family together closer than it had ever been. Ron renegotiated his definition of professional success, and altered his view that his earning power dictated his ability to be a supportive husband or a good father. By renegotiating their relationship with money and reinventing a more grounded, financially responsible lifestyle, the whole family was able to use the transition forced upon them by Ron's job loss to negotiate an exciting new beginning.

Ron and Barb discovered that Seligman was right: What makes us happy changes all the time. What keeps us fulfilled—our commitment to others, our efforts to do something meaningful, our time with family—remains constant.

Chapter 10

Division of Labor: Foregoing Assumptions, Finding Harmony

"It's your turn to clean the bathroom."

"I did it last time!"

"You did not, I did. And the time before that, too. You always have a reason why you can't do it."

"I pulled a muscle. I couldn't bend over the tub. Besides, you do it better."

"I can't believe you like living in filth."

"Filth? I'm not the one who leaves the laundry to mildew in the washing machine because I'm too lazy to transfer it to the dryer."

Sound familiar? Conversations like these echo through millions of households every day. The battle over the toilet bowl brush has been raging since before Carol Channing recited "Housework" in the 1970s album *Free to Be . . . You and Me* that celebrated gender neutrality. The poem exhorted children to remember that the lady they saw cheerily doing the housework in the television commercial was only smiling because she was an actress getting a paycheck. In the end, she advises kids that if they want life to be "sunny as summer weather," the whole family should share the burden of housework.

The poem does not, unfortunately, leave instructions for determining just how the division of labor should be apportioned, which means the weather in many couples' homes gets pretty stormy when the subject of who does what around the house comes up—unless they have negotiated a mutually acceptable arrangement.

Changing the Rules

Earlier generations had it easy. When Mary Ellen and Biff married in 1950 at the age of twenty and twenty-three respectively, they were more than likely prepared to fall into the same gender roles they had witnessed their parents and grandparents play. The wife would take care of all household duties, shopping, decorating, cooking, cleaning, and childcare. The husband would be the breadwinner, handle the finances, and be the fix it man when something broke down around the house. Then the sexual revolution came around and all the rules changed. Of course this freed both women and men to expand their horizons and pursue avenues that had long been denied them. But it also made the division of labor a lot less cut and dried at home, and doubly so in two-earner households.

An Easy Negotiation

Young marriages are extremely susceptible to divorce because there are so many points of negotiation that cannot be anticipated beforehand and the couple can take too long to recognize when a renegotiation of their original contract is in order. Not so with division of labor. Keeping the house clean, cooking, dog walking, bill paying—with perhaps the exception of the most committed slacker—people take care of these responsibilities whether they're single or married. How they do these jobs might take a little finessing to make everyone happy, but figuring out who does what, and when, can be done as soon as a couple moves in together.

Tod and Annie

When Tod and Annie got married, they were twenty-nine and thirty, respectively, and each working eighteen-hour days in the investment banking industry. They were children of broken homes. Annie was the daughter of two lawyers whose marriage broke up when Annie's mother decided she'd had it with being a career-driven supermom and left to join a commune in California. Seven-year-old Tod's mother left his father after being unable to abide by the strict gender roles demanded by his modern Muslim family. Both Tod and Annie acknowledged that their parents' second marriages were far happier and less contentious than their firsts and chalked the difference up to the parents' having a better idea of what they wanted in a husband or wife, and being better able to establish their expectations early on in their relationships.

Tod and Annie felt they had an advantage over their parents in that they had already known each other for eight years by the time they got engaged and were not afraid to voice their opinions. But they were still anxious to do whatever they could to safeguard their new marriage from the conflict that unfair divisions of labor had caused in their early home lives. Therefore, they made a premarital vow to maximize joy and minimize conflict by working out a fair division-of-labor plan.

The Division-of-Labor Plan

Negotiating your hopes and expectations regarding housework and childcare in writing before you get married or cohabitate doesn't sound romantic, but it's a great way to launch your life together. As you now recognize, your contract will be subject to change, but at least you will start off knowing exactly where you both stand. A division of labor renegotiation is one of the easiest to adjust when the time is right if you can use your original agreement as a jumping-off point.

Make a List

Start by listing every single chore and responsibility you can imagine that must be done to keep your family running smoothly. You might include getting the kids ready for school or mopping the floors. Annie and Tod's catalog included small jobs like cleaning the kitty litter and changing the air-conditioning vents, and bigger tasks like walking the dog, doing the grocery shopping, planning meals, and doing the taxes.

Rank Your List

Make a duplicate of your record so that each of you has a copy, and spend a few days alone with it to give it serious thought. Rank each chore in order of importance, then mark which ones you like to do best.

Come Together

Schedule a time to sit down with your spouse and trade lists. Now you can see whether you both believe that you should be able to eat off the floor of your kitchen, or if a biweekly sweep and mop job will suffice. Maybe you'll find that your spouse loves to water the plants, which is great because you didn't even think to include plant watering on your list.

But maybe you'll find that though mopping the kitchen floor is the tenth item on your list, below making the bed and recycling, your spouse wants the kitchen floors mopped every day. When there is a large discrepancy between what you think is important, you have to role-play. Take turns pretending you are on an airplane with an attractive stranger. Then, with the same respect, patience, and tolerance you would use in such a situation, find out why this "stranger" believes mopping the floors is so important. Do not end the conversation until you clearly understand where your spouse is coming from.

Take Two

Now that you understand each other's reasoning, renegotiate the importance of each task to your mutual satisfaction.

Play the Lottery

Flip a coin to decide who gets to make the first choice. The winner gets first pick at his favorite task. Then the other person gets to pick. The process continues until each chore has been assigned.

Plan to revisit your agreement every six months or maybe on each other's birthdays, to make sure that it is still working for both of you. Big changes such as the arrival of a child, adoption of a pet, or a job loss should be an automatic trigger to adjust your division-of-labor plan. These precautionary measures will ensure that neither of you build up the kind of resentment that can so often stress a marriage.

A Surprising Pitfall: The Closeness Bias

Annie and Tod's maturity and foresight to negotiate how they would run their home before their wedding day gave them a leg up on beating the odds of divorce for young marriages. Interestingly, however, the other factor they thought they had in their favor—that they had known each other for so long, as many modern couples do before marrying—actually put them at a disadvantage and made their initial negotiations a little rockier than expected.

Unlike the 1950s couple Mary Ellen and Biff, by the time Tod and Annie got engaged they had lived on their own for a few years, giving them ample time to establish their individual identities, as well as the quirks, routines, and habits that would need to be reconciled when they finally moved in together. After almost eight years together, Annie and Tod's relationship felt safe and comfortable. They liked to say they were each other's "BFF"—best friends forever. They knew each other so well, they thought, they could practically read each other's minds. And that, unbeknownst to them, was their weakness.

Your wife says languidly, "I'm so hot!" Coy, amorous advance, or simply a hint to turn up the air conditioner? Several studies, the results of which were published in a January 2011 issue of the *Journal of Experimental Social Psychology*, reveal that statistically, your chances of interpreting her meaning correctly are the same as if she were a stranger. Research has shown that the closer we feel to someone, the less inclined we are to share all the information we know, and the more inclined we are to assume we understand her. Our belief that our shared history allows our partners—or other people we feel close to—to fill in the blanks is called the closeness bias.

In fact, married people don't communicate with each other any better than they do with perfect strangers. In some cases, they communicate *better* with strangers, because they don't assume that strangers know everything they know; they automatically communicate more information because there is no closeness bias. Yet married people consistently overestimate their ability to convey their meaning to their spouses, and they overestimate their ability to understand their partners' meaning, as well.

Because of their closeness bias, Tod assumed that Annie had to have an immaculate kitchen but didn't care so much about the state of her bedroom, because he noticed that she tended to throw her clothes on the floor before falling into bed at night when they stayed in her apartment. Annie had seen Tod's trashed bachelor pad and assumed that he didn't really care if his home was a mess. But in fact, he did; he just didn't have enough time to clean up the way he would have liked to. It actually bugged him to see Annie's clothes in a pile, but he did not feel comfortable saying anything because it wasn't his home, and he knew what his own apartment looked like. If they had moved in together without negotiating first, it's almost guaranteed they would have started bickering.

Because they took a proactive approach to their relationship, though, the early years of their marriage have been relatively smooth sailing. They credit their marital harmony to their family mantra: "What I know is different from what you know."

Chapter 11

Hobbies: Championing Each Other's Changing Interests

As we've established, we desire people who are enthusiastic and curious, who want to be a part of our world but who can also expose us to new horizons and experiences. Sometimes you fall in love over a shared passion—you regularly spot each other dressed up in full medieval regalia at Renaissance festivals, or you have repeated run-ins on the hiking trail.

On occasion it's the fact that a person's hobbies or interests are different from yours that sparks romantic feelings—you have no artistic talent but are entranced by the beautiful ceramics she makes in her spare time; you're both accountants but you love that his secret ambition is to become a screenplay writer. These interests are part of what define your partner and may even help character-ize your relationship. That's why whether we share the same pas-sions or merely enjoy how our spouse's hobbies make his eyes light up, it can be disappointing when he abandons a once-cherished activity. It can be especially stressful on a relationship when it's the very thing that drew you together or has always served as a bond-ing experience.

Negotiating So No One Gets Left Behind

As we've mentioned, when we are the ones instigating change, we feel in control. When our spouse does it, it can provoke anxiety. Trudy was beside herself when her husband Boris told her he no longer wanted to play bridge. They had been bridge partners for years and had developed a large circle of friends through the game. Trudy was surprised when Boris started dragging his feet before going to games but never dreamed he would lose interest entirely. When he finally told her he didn't want to play anymore, she demanded to know why. He couldn't offer a real reason; he was just bored and wanted to do something else, maybe building model airplanes like his buddy Nick. Trudy was stunned and hurt. This was their "thing," their social anchor. What would people think? Was Boris going to find her boring, too? And why would anyone want to build an airplane?

Seven Steps to Renegotiating a Shared Interest or Activity

Ideally, marriage shouldn't constrict two horizons into a single limited one, but merge them into one that is greater than the sum of its parts. By following the tips below, you can ensure that your relationship is a source of freedom of expression and joyful companionship, not a straitjacket.

1. Don't take it personally. There's no reason to try to extrapolate a bigger meaning out of your partner's decision. It's perfectly natural for people's interests to wax and wane. Newness breeds desire, as you recall. Try to look at your spouse's shifting interests as an opportunity to spice up your life together. Boris's decision to stop playing bridge was just that, a decision to quit a card game, not a desire to quit his relationship with Trudy.

2. Refrain from critical judgment. Just because you don't see the value or merit in building model airplanes, video games, knitting, or whatever new interest has piqued your partner's imagination doesn't mean you have the right to demean it. Stay positive.

3. Force yourself to show enthusiasm in your partner's fresh attention, even if you have to fake it. Ask questions to learn more about it. Find out what inspired him to try this particular activity. Encourage him to enjoy the effort he spends on it, even if you feel like it's taking time away from you. This can require effort, especially when your spouse takes up something that demands a lot of training, such as a triathlon, which can absorb up to twenty hours of swimming, biking, and running per week.

4. Discuss your feelings. So your wife has lost interest in gardening and you miss having a yard that is the showplace of the neighborhood. Say so in a way that conveys your gratitude for her past achievements, but doesn't try to make her feel guilty for moving on. You might say something like, "Honey, I loved the way the house looked in springtime, when the flowers came up. If you're not interested in gardening, what do you think about our hiring someone to plant some new ones, or teach me how to plant for next season?"

5. Make plans of your own. If you support your spouse in his or her choices, your partner will probably extend the same courtesy to you. Trudy had to accept that she was losing her bridge collaborator, but she couldn't let him take away her pleasure in the game and the social opportunities it provided. Ultimately, she told Boris that though he was still her first choice, she was going to ask her neighbor to be her partner and he would have to fend for himself on the evenings she was out playing bridge.

6. Set limits. Hobbies are a means to enhance life, not detract from it. Neither spouse should have a diversion that seriously undermines the health of the marriage. If your wife is obsessed

with photography, agree on an amount of time that could work for her to spend taking pictures away from home. It's much easier to support each other's interests when they don't threaten to supplant the marriage.

7. Find some common ground. Look for the new opportunities your partner's interest can afford you. Many policemen were part of Boris's model-building club that met weekly to fly the airplanes in the town fields. Once Trudy let down her guard, she found that she enjoyed getting to know them and their wives. Boris was touched by her efforts to be a good sport. Remembering that Trudy had often talked about how much fun it would be to join a supper club, he took the initiative and joined so that they would have prescheduled couple time together. Whether it's sharing a weekly candlelit dinner for two or taking bike rides after work, it's imperative that you renegotiate to find an activity that you both enjoy. Remember that it's a great way to keep your desire alive and the paths of communication open.

Negotiating When the Choice Is Not Your Own

It's not always by preference that we have to stop doing something that we love. When we're forced to abandon a hobby or sport that we shared with our spouse because of illness, injury, or age, the amount of turmoil that may arise can be surprising. You could discover that an activity you shared helped mediate certain feelings and dynamics that you only recognize now in its absence. Max and Debbie found themselves in just this situation.

Max and Debbie

Max and Debbie met at a ski resort in Colorado. Max was impressed by how Debbie tackled the difficult slopes fearlessly, while Debbie loved how Max tried to keep up with her, despite her superior skills. For ten years, the two had a great partnership and looked forward to winter, when they would go skiing with friends. They'd ski all day, eat delicious meals with the gang, and then retire to their room to make love. No matter what troubles they faced, Max and Debbie could usually resolve their problems after a day on the slopes, feeling united over their shared enthusiasm.

Then Max began to develop knee problems and his doctor insisted that he stop skiing to curtail further damage to his joints. Max was sick at the prospect of telling Debbie his news. How would she react when she learned he could no longer ski?

Debbie expressed nothing but concern and compassion. Of course she didn't want him to jeopardize his health for the sake of a sport. She assured him that it wasn't a big deal.

When the Christmas holidays approached, however, Debbie realized that going skiing was not an option. She couldn't go and just leave Max alone in the lodge all day. Until then, Debbie hadn't processed how Max's affliction would affect her. Now, instead of hitting the slopes over the holidays, they'd have to spend it with one of their families, like every other boring couple.

Though she knew it wasn't his fault, Debbie began to resent Max. He suddenly seemed weak and diminished, no longer the virile, sporty man with whom she had fallen in love Max, already feeling vulnerable and embarrassed by his condition, sensed his wife's resentment and began withdrawing. When she'd return home in the evening, he'd hardly move from the brown chair where he liked to read. Contact was minimal.

Pretty soon, the two were fighting over trivial matters. The quarreling became so bad they started sleeping in separate bedrooms.

Max's and Debbie's problems arose because their changed agreement over how to spend the holidays had brought to light two implicit contracts they'd forged in the early days of their relationship:

1. Until then, Debbie led and Max followed. Now Max's needs were dominating their relationship and Debbie was having a hard time accepting her loss of control.
2. Max had always felt a little inferior to Debbie, and now his injury had made him feel even more so. He had slipped into a low-grade depression.

On the surface, their problem seemed insurmountable—each had fallen in love with a fit athlete and their implicit contract was grounded in a spirit of friendly competition that was no longer possible.

If you are in this situation, do not despair. Over the years you have built up a lifetime of memories, quite apart from your favorite activity. It is on those recollections of shared enjoyment that you will renegotiate the foundation of your future.

Five Steps to Renegotiate the Activity You Love

Renegotiating our hobbies or interests may not seem as important to the health of our relationships as something like a job loss or the decision of whether or not to have children, but it can be. Treat your and you partner's hobbies with the seriousness and respect they deserve. The following five steps will help:

Recognize Your Value

You are not what you do. It's your inherent qualities and talents that made you a skilled athlete or brilliant performer. You still have those qualities even if you can't play or perform anymore. There's no reason you can't channel them into something new. The inventive part is figuring out what that something will be.

Understand What the Activities Represent

A lot of Debbie's love for the ski vacations she shared with Max stemmed from the fact that it helped her defy her parent's expectations of what married adulthood should look like. Skiing had helped her to individuate from the stultifying box she felt they'd tried to stick her in when she was growing up. But if she couldn't open her mind to new avenues, eventually her beloved sport would become the new stultifying box.

Explore What Gives You Pleasure

Write a long list of what feelings the activity evokes in you, and what you love best about it. Funny enough, when Debbie and Max shared their list, they found that they had listed the same things: the excitement, the adventure, the fresh air, the sense of camaraderie.

Prioritize

Compare your lists. Max and Debbie laughed when they saw that they had prioritized what was important to them in the same order. The list made them laugh for five minutes and realize that, instead of their relationship being hierarchical, it was very much a harmony of two people being on the same emotional page.

Consider Other Activities with Similar Qualities

List what other activities could most closely match all the qualities on your lists. Max and Debbie both came up with other group sports that could offer the emotional high that skiing provided, such as sailing, scuba diving, and snowmobiling.

Making the lists allowed Debbie and Max to affirm themselves and each other again, and rekindled their physical and emotional desires as they conjured up the new possibilities that awaited them.

Negotiating When Your Interests Draw You Apart

Often the activities that we love no longer suit us once we move into a new chapter of our lives. Couples facing major transitions like a new baby, an impending empty nest, or retirement, are particularly vulnerable if they don't realize that they must renegotiate their expectations of each other as they enter a new life phase.

Rajiv and Melissa

When they met, Rajiv and Melissa were each rising stars in the financial industry. After six months of an intensive courtship, they decided to get married. Both kept working until Melissa gave birth to their first child. After much discussion, the couple decided Rajiv would keep working while Melissa stayed home to raise their son. Melissa enjoyed being a stay-at-home mom, but felt her creative skills were going to waste. She started experimenting in the kitchen and making elaborate gourmet meals. Rajiv was delighted and had fun inviting his colleagues over for lavish dinners, proud to show off his wife's culinary skills.

As time went on Rajiv and Melissa had two more children. Their lives were busy and happy. Rajiv continued to move up the ladder of success while Melissa held down the home front, volunteering at the kids' school and continuing to develop her cooking skills. Eventually, as the children grew old enough to find their entertainment in their own social lives, the big family dinners they once enjoyed became a fond memory. Slowly, Melissa realized she no longer took pleasure in creating meals for just one or two people. Her interests drifted to fashion. Instead of fixing big dinners, Melissa channeled her energy into making her own clothes, losing herself for hours in the small closet she turned into an atelier.

Rajiv and Melissa's oldest child went away to college, and the other two were busy with after-school activities, dates, and other teenage pursuits. By this time, Rajiv was ready to take an early retirement. After spending the past twenty years working and providing a comfortable lifestyle for his family, he expected a hero's welcome. Instead, he was met with an indifferent wife and mostly absent children. It was especially galling that Melissa no longer seemed interested in cooking his favorite food, preferring to pull together light meals for herself or go out to dinner.

The tension grew in their household to the point that Rajiv and Melissa realized if they didn't get help their marriage wouldn't last four days past their youngest child's high school graduation. By the time the couple came to my office, they were barely on speaking terms.

When asked to explain his feelings, Rajiv vented for several minutes and finally spat, "Melissa spends all her time with that stupid sewing machine. I worked like a dog for twenty years to give her a nice life and it's like I don't even count." Melissa's reaction was equally fierce. "How can he accuse me of neglect when I dedicated my whole life to raising our children and supporting him and his career? Apparently, cooking is an acceptable hobby because it serves his needs, but fashion isn't because it has nothing to do with him."

Rajiv and Melissa didn't know it yet, but they were suffering from the same problem. To get to the heart of it, they needed to acknowledge that their marriage was transitioning to a new phase, and find a way to renegotiate their expectations of each other so they could adjust.

Write a Script

Both Rajiv and Melissa were impressively articulate and self-aware, yet each was so wrapped up in outrage and self-righteousness neither could hear what the other was trying to say. To force them to listen to each other, I wrote down what they told me and drafted a sample script for each of them so they could discuss their feelings in a calmer way.

Melissa's Script

"Honey, I want you to know how grateful I am for how hard you have worked over the years. I know it wasn't easy spending long hours at the office. Thanks to you, we were able to afford a beautiful home and send our family to great schools. I'm really proud of you. The thing is, while you were at work, I was busy, too. I had to be. Sacrificing my career to take care of the kids left a big hole in my life. I realized if I didn't fill it, I'd become resentful. That's why I started cooking. I really enjoyed feeding you and the children, but I also did it for myself, to stretch my creative talent. Now that our lives have changed, I want to evolve differently. Making clothes is a way to do something nice for myself that doesn't involve caring for anyone else. That may sound selfish, but for the past twenty years, I've been the caretaker for this family. Now I want to put my own needs first. That doesn't mean I don't love you, but it does mean things have changed around here, and I would like you to support me."

Rajiv's Script

"Darling, I am proud of the home you worked so hard to make for us. I know it was a big sacrifice for you to quit work for the sake of the kids and I'm grateful. But while you were busy at home, I was spending most of my time at the office in an extremely stressful environment. It was hard to put in long hours while you guys seemed to be having so much fun without me. Coming home from work and smelling your fabulous cooking, though, made it all worthwhile. Now that I'm through working so hard, I miss the feeling of coming home to a loving wife and a good meal. For me, food is love. When you don't prepare it, I feel rejected. I understand you like to make clothes, but is there any way we can recapture that feeling of looking out for each other again? I really miss that."

Both wanted to be recognized for their unique contributions and talents, but each felt belittled for them. I instructed both to rewrite their scripts any way they liked, so long as they refrained from assigning blame or shame. After they tweaked the scripts a bit, Rajiv and Melissa read them aloud to each other. It felt funny, but reading the scripts helped Rajiv and Melissa in two ways:

1. Demanding that your partner stay silent while you read out loud ensures that she will stay focused on your words, and not on her rebuttal. If she can't interrupt, attack, or defend herself, she can't distract you from making your point calmly and rationally.

2. These scripts don't just outline Rajiv's and Melissa's grievances; they identify their needs. Melissa needs to feel celebrated and supported; Rajiv needs to feel rewarded and nurtured. Once they'd established what was really troubling them they could take steps to finding a solution that got both of them what they wanted. Now Rajiv takes great pride in running Melissa's fashion line, while Melissa takes pleasure in fixing elaborate holiday meals that bring the whole family together in a spirit of harmony several times a year.

Chapter 12

Changing Values: Respecting Your Differences

We often choose mates whose value systems for the most part mirror our own, and rarely do we consider the possibility that someday they might not. Couples who meet at a Greenpeace protest or pro-life rally would probably feel secure in assuming that their values and politics will forever match. Even when there are significant differences between people overall, so long as both partners respect the other's values, such differences needn't cause friction. The problem is, however, that people's values are defined and refined over a lifetime. Your feelings about education funding when you are a twenty-one-year-old college student could change drastically once you become a homeowner. Your fervent condemnation of homosexuality could be altered if your daughter comes out.

Anything is possible as we grow older and new experiences shape and color our views of the world. No couple, no matter how passionately the two have bonded over mutually shared politics and value systems, can guarantee that they will always see eye to eye. And sometimes our spouse can change his values in such a way as to actually offend our own. When that happens, it's a serious breach of the couple's contract. But though a problem like this may seem insurmountable, it can be renegotiated if you can draw on a deep understanding of how people form commitments and learn to love.

How We Become Committed Adults

In a thirty-year analysis of development from birth to adulthood, scientists found that two factors prevail in determining whether an adult forms a strong sense of commitment: first, the presence of a supportive, involved mother during toddlerhood, and second, the opportunity to develop the ability to work through conflict in adolescence. A person backed by this winning combination is invariably a "strong link" in adult relationships—someone who is firmly committed to staying the course and not easily persuaded to abandon his or her efforts.

Because changing values can cause such a deep rift in a relationship, knowing whether you and your partner are weak or strong links will affect how you negotiate your way through the transition. When both partners are strong links, they will have a solid stake in continuing the relationship. Obviously that's a good thing. The downside is that when couples with this level of commitment experience conflict, it tends to be more explosive and violent than in couples where the members are both weak links—individuals who might be more likely to consider leaving the relationship than fighting for it. Paradoxically, two weak links may not be as committed to working things out, but their expectations are lower, too, which means their conflicts are less volatile and more easily negotiated, which can help their relationship last.

Negotiation 101 ————————————————————————

Knowing whether you and your partner are weak or strong links will help you determine how fierce your renegotiations are likely to be. Did you have a loving home life while growing up? Do you form secure, anxious, or insecure attachments? (See Chapter 1 for a refresher on the types of attachments and their implications.) How were your adolescent friendships? Were you a loner, on sports teams, one of the popular kids, or a nerd? Were you able to have conflicts and then make up and go on with the friendships? Or did you fight and never speak again?

If your partner is a strong link but you are a weak link then the longevity of your coupledom rests in your hands. The weak link holds the power in a relationship because walking away is not as big of a deal as it is to a strong link. If this is you, you'll need to work against your history and consciously help yourself develop a more secure feeling to give your relationship its best chance of survival.

Kara and Raphael

Kara and Rafe grew up in the same small North Carolina town. Both came from staunch Democratic families who could trace their lineage to the founding of their home state and had been active in town politics since before America was ratified. Though they had crossed paths in their youth, Kara and Rafe didn't meet again until after college graduation, when they found themselves working for the same congressional representative in Washington, D.C. They fell in love and married in a town wedding that could have been a small Democratic national convention.

After several years of raising three children in expensive D.C., Raphael began to think that working for the government was too much of a charitable enterprise. He and Kara agreed that, though it would require some sacrifice, he should go back to school and become a lawyer.

Five years later, Raphael was working for a conservative white-shoe law firm in Washington. Slowly, he realized that he was beginning to concur with many of his Republican colleagues about the causes of the problems facing the country, and their solutions. As his political allegiance shifted, tensions began to grow between him and Kara. The night he came home to tell her that he had joined a political action group dedicated to seeking out and backing the ideal Republican candidate in the next election, Kara, who worked near the Oval Office as a liaison between the press and the president, slept on the couch. She couldn't imagine being married to a Republican; she'd as soon marry a Martian.

Negotiating with a Strong Link

Kara was horrified by her husband's about-face, but she was also a strong link. And so was Raphael, which means that while their emotions would surely run high, they both had the motivation and determination to go through a negotiation for as long as it took to get their marriage back on track.

Ideally, the partner who has initiated the breach in contract should focus the negotiation on making his spouse feel heard, and getting his motives and intentions across.

1. Clear your mind and listen. Stop worrying about proving your point or trying to convince your partner you are right. Give your spouse ample time to explain why she is so upset by your choices or change of heart. As Kara vented, she finally hit on something that made complete sense to Raphael: She needed to know that she was married to someone who had the nation and its citizens' best interest at heart.
2. When you finally get why your spouse is so upset, repeat what you think you understand.
3. Then ask, "Did I get what you were trying to say?" If so, move on to the next step. If not, ask her to explain herself again. Repeat this exchange until she is convinced you understand.

4. Now that you know what is at the heart of your partner's feelings, you can build a bridge.
5. You are not the only one who needs to understand, of course. In order for your marriage to move forward without this issue undermining it, your spouse must go through the same process to understand you.

For example, Kara believed that Rafe was turning against their families, their town, their ancestors, and their historical patriotic truths. As she began truly to listen to him, however, she understood that Rafe believed he was not going against his heritage at all. He was, on the contrary, changing his ideas on the best way to support the values his ancestors and Kara's fought for so long ago. As Kara began to see that, though Rafe was no longer a left-leaning liberal, he was still the same loving, compassionate man she adored, her truculent stance softened. She realized that being financially secure, having a vibrant sex life, and being married to a loyal husband and involved father was far more important to her than being married to a Democrat.

Ultimately, Kara and Raphael negotiated that they would simply agree to have different politics and would use each other as a resource to help explore important issues from all sides.

Negotiating with a Weak Link

When a weak link and a strong link marry, the negotiations must be approached differently. Jackie and David were happily married for thirty-five years. They had raised their children in a calm, religious household, and in fact, their strong religious faith had helped them successfully negotiate through the minor challenges life had handed them so far. That is, until Jackie, an oncologist who had worked for years in a large hospital, mentioned to David that after seeing too many people die because of the insufficient number of healthy organs available for transplant, she had decided to be an organ donor. David was shocked. Their religion was very clear: the human body was sacred, and had to be buried intact in a grave. Jackie was sure that in time David would come around. He was a good man; surely he could see how her decision supported their faith's exhortations to help the weak and the suffering. Unfortunately, there was something she didn't know about David that would make it very difficult for her to successfully negotiate with him

The Weak Link

It is not a couple's individual commitments that determine whether the two will stay together during tough times, but how well their levels of commitments match up. David was a weak link. His mother had died when he was a toddler, so there was no supportive maternal presence in his babyhood. His father moved the family several times during his adolescence, so he never had time to make close friends with whom he could practice resolving conflicts.

Although he loved Jackie, because of his background, David was ill-prepared to consider putting in the work it would take to negotiate what he perceived as Jackie's public affront to his family values. And he had the power—when a weak link and a strong link pair up, the one less invested has more influence on the relationship.

A strong link will usually find a way toward benevolence and tolerance in the midst of marital conflict, like Kara did. A weak link, however, may already have one foot out the door. David wasn't a coward so much as he was hopeless that he and Jackie could resolve the conflict. Raphael was upset by Kara's reaction to his changing political views and saw she had no intention of changing her mind, but she believed there had to be a way for them to build a bridge back to each other. Nothing in David's life experience led him to suppose that it was possible to build such a bridge back to Jackie; maybe it was best to just move on.

Two Preliminary Negotiations

David could not expect Jackie to be a mind reader. She did not have any idea that her decision had compelled him to question whether he could stay in the marriage, or if he needed to find a partner who would more closely share his values. He would have to communicate with her—clearly and resolutely—that his religious beliefs meant he had to judge her decision to donate her organs as unacceptable.

For her part, Jackie had to decide whether her conviction in organ donation was worth jeopardizing her marriage. In the end, she could not bend to David's will over a decision that to her was so clearly in line with their beliefs. Had she not learned about how to negotiate with a weak link that would have probably been the end of the marriage. Instead, Jackie took the following steps:

1. Accept.

She accepted David's weak link status and did not take it personally that he had so quickly considered ending their marriage. This went a long way toward keeping her from letting her anger or hurt affect the way she communicated with him.

2. Get to the heart of things.

She began to study what was truly bothering David. She realized that his violent reaction was in part because he felt that she had completed her decision without consulting him, and he feared she was on a slippery slope to becoming less religiously observant. To make up for that oversight, she asked him to join her in couples' counseling with one of their religious leaders, who happened to be an ethicist. The additional guidance of a third party would help her weak-link husband feel like his concerns were being taken seriously. That, in turn, gave him more incentive to be more open-minded. He agreed to let Jackie educate him about the subject by taking him to films, by introducing him to people who needed organ transplants, and educating him in any way she could.

3. Offer support without compromising yourself.

Ultimately Jackie's decision became a moot point as they gained an increasing closeness to one another. David never changed his mind, but he fell in love with Jackie again and realized he would be a fool to leave her. Their sex improved, their humor returned, and life was never better.

Part 3

Renegotiating How to Cherish One Another

Taking care of your partner is the ultimate act of kindness and love. The best way to take care of your partner, however, is to take good care of yourself. When you feel strong, healthy, independent, and confident, you're not a source of worry or an insatiable hole that your partner feels compelled to try to fill. It's important, of course, to show that you need each other, and that each of you provides the other with love and support that no one else could; but you can need each other without dragging each other down with neediness. Every chapter that follows offers advice on how to take care of yourself when facing challenging times so that you are emotionally strong enough to take care of your spouse when he or she needs you.

Chapter 13

Infertility: Preventing Your Marriage from Becoming Barren

Infertility is one of the cruelest blows a couple can face. And over the past few decades, more and more have had to face it. According to Sandra Glahn and William Cutrer's book, *When Empty Arms Become a Heavy Burden*, approximately 10 million people in the United States are unable to procreate after a year or more of regular sexual relations—that's one in six Americans of childbearing age.

It's not just heartbreaking; it's infuriating. The Rolling Stones sing, "You Can't Always Get What You Want," but we live in a culture that assures us that if you try hard enough, you can, in fact, do just that.

Couples are shocked and baffled that they can do everything right and still not succeed. It's a situation many people find almost unbearable, and it can take a massive toll on a relationship. Negotiating through infertility is a delicate endeavor, but there are steps you can take to avoid hurting each other and safeguard your marriage as you wade through these difficult waters.

If you are struggling with infertility, or if you ever have to navigate the process of deciding how to proceed through this complex and emotional journey, make sure to do two important things.

Introduce New Experiences Into Your Relationship

Couples who are trying to have a baby can become obsessed and talk about nothing else. And although they're having sex all the time, they're not necessarily making love, which can weaken their emotional connection. Introduce a new experience into your life so that you stay bonded. During what is likely to be an emotional time, you want your levels of oxytocin, the bonding hormone, to be as high as you can possibly get them. Learn to play tennis, take a pottery class, meditate together, do anything, but do it together and carve out special time to focus on something other than whether or not children are going to be a part of your lives.

No matter what decisions you will be forced to negotiate, the bonding experience of doing something new together will help keep your negotiations calm and smooth. In addition, the pleasure you get in participating in a new activity jointly will remind you that together you form a great partnership, with or without children.

Live in a State of Mindful Presence

It can be very easy to get swallowed up in your own thoughts and emotions when struggling with infertility, but when you live with mindful presence, you're aware of your feelings, including the negative ones, while still being acutely alert to everything that is good around you. With mindful presence, you can have dark moments, feel sad, and even have self-pity, but you are still able to see that there is beauty in the world and that you have a lot to offer it. This vision gives you a feeling of self-love, which helps you be gentle with yourself. The gentler you are with yourself, the gentler you can be with your spouse, and the easier it is to remember that whatever you're going through, he or she is going through it too. When partners make a conscious choice to be mindfully present, they are able to reduce their stress and increase feelings of hope and optimism.

Developing Mindful Presence ——————————————

Meditation, tai chi, and yoga are three mind-body spiritual practices that can usher mindful presence into your life.

The other huge benefit to mindful presence is that it helps you keep from getting stuck in rigid beliefs that can block your flexibility and cut you off from options that you might not have previously considered. People have beliefs, and they have goals, and too often their beliefs get in the way of their goals. The more you are prepared to approach negotiations with an open mind, the better your chance of sustaining your marriage and creating the family of your dreams.

When you live with mindful presence you can:

- Empathically connect with compassion and understanding to yourself and partner.
- Face fears of rejection or inadequacy.
- Protect yourself from acting out of fear.
- Be curious about and find validity in other people's perspective.
- Convey honor and respect for yourself and others.
- Consciously act in ways that let your partner know your sincere interest, love, and commitment.
- Treat yourself and your partner with dignity, even when he or she hurts or angers you.

Clearly, when we are mindfully present, we are well equipped to navigate the important and possibly difficult decisions that might be up ahead when the baby you so desperately want doesn't arrive as soon as you might have hoped.

Edith and Nicholas

Edith and Nicholas both came from large families. When they met and married the clans could not have been happier. All of the wedding toasts celebrated how wonderful it would be when they brought more children into the family. And what incredible children they were destined to be! Edith was a top-winning state champion swimmer who had secured a college swimming scholarship. Nicholas was a triple-threat jock, playing hockey, soccer, and track with equal brilliance. His soccer skills had earned him a college scholarship, too. The two athletes married and couldn't wait for the babies to show up. They waited. And waited. After five years of trying and waiting, their marriage was deteriorating rapidly.

While everyone's experience with infertility is unique, there are six phases most will go through should they opt to pursue medical help in conceiving a child.

These phases are:

- The dawning phase
- The mobilization phase
- The early- and middle-immersion phase
- The later-immersion phase
- The resolution phase
- The legacy phase

You can find out more detailed information on these phases in the book *Couple Therapy for Infertility*, by Ronny Diamond et al. Being aware of each of these phases can be instrumental in helping you avoid some of infertility's pitfalls and give you perspective when you're negotiating with your partner. If you start to fight, or feel depressed, think about what phase you might be in. This will help you keep in mind that you are not alone and that your feelings are normal. Let's look at some ways you can negotiate through each of these phases.

Negotiating the Dawning Phase

This initial phase is where the first point of negotiation occurs, when couples finally admit that they have a problem and will need to find a fertility specialist. Getting to the point that both members of the couple are willing to face facts isn't always easy. Often one spouse will resist getting help because he can't bear the feelings of humiliation and inadequacy that might accompany the admission that only a medical procedure will allow him to conceive a child. He may feel shame about his body, or point the finger at his spouse to deflect any blame he feels will be placed on him.

If you or your spouse is having difficulty coming to terms during the dawning phase, try to renegotiate the idea that infertility is shameful by sharing your feelings as openly as possible. Show your vulnerability, and encourage your spouse to talk to you about his or her feelings, even if what they say might hurt. You cannot control people, but you can influence them by making them feel less alone. You dilute shame by putting feelings into words. Harboring shame is like harboring an enemy. Shame is the most debilitating of all the emotions because it paralyzes you, which is the worst thing that can happen when time is precious and decisions need to be made.

Edith and Nick were in such incredible physical shape that it took them longer than average to admit that they were facing infertility and needed help. Unfortunately, the stress they experienced during this period of denial had a direct effect on their increasing marital conflict. As their sex becomes a chore fraught with anticipation and frustration, they began to turn on each other for insignificant things, and eventually turned away from each other, though they still timed their lovemaking for Edith's most fertile phase of the month. Edith, in particular, personalized the problem as a sign of her own inadequacy and uselessness. She withdrew from all the activities she once loved, and resented Nick for his seeming ability to continue with life as usual when the future seemed so empty and hopeless. Didn't he care that they couldn't have children?

Nick finally approached his wife and said to her, "Edith, I want a baby with you more than anything, but I want to bring that baby into a happy home. We can't keep up like this. I hate the idea of going through doctors to get our child, but if in the end we bring home a baby, don't you think it will have been worth the effort? I'll try anything so long as it's with you by my side." With that, Edith was able to see that her husband was just as frightened as she was and was able to let go of her shame and her unfair assumptions about what her husband was feeling. She knew that regardless of what happened, their marriage would be her safe haven. With that in mind, she and Nick were calmly and lovingly able to negotiate the decisions that arose during all of the phases that came next.

Negotiating the Mobilization Phase

Once a couple has discussed the problem and been evaluated by a fertility specialist, the two are generally introduced to their medical options. In Nick and Edith's case, they were given two, in vitro fertilization (IVF) or intrauterine insemination, which required them to go home and negotiate. Nick wanted to go straight to the IVF procedure, while Edith was resistant to the surgery if she could just take hormones to jumpstart the production of more eggs and be artificially inseminated with Nick's sperm, a far less invasive process. Though Nick would have preferred a more aggressive approach, once he more clearly understood Edith's fear of surgery, he agreed to try intrauterine insemination first.

Negotiating the Early- and Middle-Immersion Phase

This is when couples typically become consumed by the topic of their infertility project. As couples try first one procedure and then another, and maybe suffer miscarriages, they are bombarded with wild swings of hope and despair, and can feel increasingly out of control. Nick and Edith, however, continued to maintain a united front when dealing with their problem, and made sure to talk through their feelings as often as possible. They were hugely disappointed when the insemination intervention did not work, but they had negotiated themselves onto the same page so well that they barely had to discuss anything before electing to engage in the IVF intervention.

Negotiating the Later-Immersion Phase

The later-immersion phase is typified by obsessive thinking, for by now there is nothing on each person's mind but baby making, baby making, baby making. As options begin to seem more limited and finances start to suffer, it can become tedious, disheartening, and cause wild swings of jealousy as couples look around at all the seemingly happy families that had no problem knocking out multiple babies.

Though remarkably resilient and positive, Nick and Edith had their dark moments, too. Their entire life was ovulation kits, sex on demand, doctors, shots, and hormones. Nick hated hearing his friends talk about their kids, and Edith felt like she'd been punched in the chest when her friend Melanie, who had also been going through IVF, announced she was pregnant.

The later-immersion phase can be extremely painful, but if you know you're in it you can take steps to negotiate how you handle it. It will not be easy, but do everything you can to find the humor in life. Watch as many funny movies as you can. Go to comedy clubs. Find any and every reason to laugh, preferably with your spouse. The more you can laugh, the more you can dilute the black bile of jealousy and the yearning for what you can't have, and the more you can negotiate with yourself to look for the silver lining if you are starting to believe that life is unfair.

Seeking out humor and laughter does not mean, however, that you should ignore your pain. You can only negotiate well if you allow yourself access to your emotions. If you deny half of yourself, the downbeat side, in a way you're only halfheartedly in the world. And when you're halfhearted, you're only half-present, making it hard to articulate what you need to talk about so you can move forward.

Negotiating the Resolution Phase

After a year, Nick and Edith entered the resolution phase. It is during this phase when couples must eventually make difficult decisions, among which are whether, and when, to end their fertility treatments; whether to adopt; or whether to choose to abandon the idea of parenthood altogether. None of these decisions can be made lightly, and all require individuals to renegotiate their relationships and their own identities.

These negotiations will take time and patience. Each one will require you to dig as deeply as possible into your own and your spouse's assumptions about what family and parenthood means to you. For example, if you are negotiating whether to adopt, you have to renegotiate your idea that being a parent means passing along your genes. So the question that you might ask is, "If our goal was to reproduce ourselves, is there still value to raising children together? Is there any other value to having children?" Whether the answer is yes or no, do not accept it immediately. Turn your answer over with your spouse; test it, question it. Only by challenging yourself to see if you can get beyond your initial principles and fixed ideas can you see that, though this door of opportunity may be shut to you, there may be another that you haven't looked at yet. Stay positive and stay open-minded. You may ultimately come right back to your first gut reaction, but at least you and your spouse will know that you explored every avenue and decided together that this was the one that was best for you both.

In the end, Nick and Edith adopted a baby from the Congo. Not long after bringing her home, they discovered that Edith was pregnant.

Negotiating the Legacy Phase

Even when couples emerge from their infertility experience with a strong union, the effects can linger. It can take a while to resurrect an enjoyable sex life now that it is no longer connected to baby making but to pleasure and love. People who have identified with infertility now must struggle to renegotiate their self-image. But if you have skillfully negotiated through something as trying and life changing as infertility, your marriage will likely remain strong as you begin this next exciting chapter. Sometimes a challenge overcome like this one leaves an empty feeling when life resumes without the stress of "against all odds."

Chapter 14

Trauma: Sticking Together After a Traumatic Event

Trauma is caused by any event that essentially destroys your ability to see the world as a safe place. Whether it's a tsunami or child abuse, whether it's a one-time event or lasts for years, there are experiences that can so terribly overwhelm a person's ability to cope that the body responds by simply shutting down. Some people re-experience the event over and over again in their minds; some become enraged and violent; some become lethargic and depressed; some use alcohol, narcotics, or sex to numb their pain and keep their minds distracted. It doesn't cause just an existential or emotional shift; trauma causes actual physical changes to the brain.

According to Daniel J. Siegel, author of *The Developing Mind*, when a person experiences trauma he may block the emotions in order to survive; but emotions play a central role in self-regulation. Self-regulation is what keeps you from acting on impulse every time you feel something; it allows you to use your intellectual override to manage your emotions. Without it, you can't communicate or negotiate well and relationships suffer. No one can hear you when your emotions are explosive. They get scared or they get defensive. Either way, the communication comes to a standstill.

If you are traumatized, part of your recovery must include learning to renegotiate your perception of how you fit into the world, your sense of trust, and your belief that your spouse can still offer you the comfort and support you need. If you are married to someone who is suffering from trauma, your negotiation efforts will center on foregoing the conviction that you can help your spouse on your own, and understanding that, though the person you love will never be the same, with your help renegotiating the effects of trauma, he or she might become even better.

Negotiation 101

Any couple coping with the effects of trauma would be well advised to get some kind of professional help. It's simply too much for most of us to try to handle this kind of negotiation all on our own. While it's important for the traumatized person to find a professional to help him understand his feelings and teach him how to manage his symptoms, he has to accept that his problems affect the rest of the family. That's why group therapy is an excellent choice—it gives a voice to both the traumatized individual and his or her spouse. In group, both can see that their feelings are not vastly different from those of their peers. The sense of community helps ease feelings of victimization, alienation, and isolation.

Figure Out Attachment Style

To figure out the best starting point for renegotiating your relationship with your traumatized spouse, it helps to appreciate how events from his past could be affecting his interpretation of and recovery from his trauma. You'll recall from Chapter 1 that there are three kinds of attachment: secure, anxious, and insecure. Securely attached adults are less likely to submit to the effects of trauma, whereas insecurely attached people often succumb to them. John Bowlby, in his book *Attachment and Loss*, lists four types of insecure attachments, each determined by how a person's parents treated him as a child:

Types of Insecure Attachment

Attachment Style	Parental Style	Adult Characteristics
Avoidant	Unavailable	Distant, intolerant
Ambivalent	Inconsistent and intrusive	Anxious, insecure, charming
Disorganized	Parental behavior frightening	Chaotic, craves security, untrusting
Reactive	Unattached, malfunction	No positive relationships

Sherry and Adam

When the aftermath of 9/11 threatened to ruin Sherry and Adam's marriage, acknowledging their respective attachment styles helped them accept each other's view of the world and renegotiate a better way to cope with stress.

Adam worked on the third floor of Tower One of the World Trade Center, and Sherry worked three blocks away. Though they knew they would always be haunted by the events of 9/11, they thought they had successfully put the worst of it behind them. That is, until the recent tenth anniversary of the violence coupled with the killing of Osama Ben Laden caused a re-traumatization for Adam. His attitude became increasingly negative. He couldn't sleep, and when he did, he had nightmares. When he bothered to talk to Sherry, he treated her, as well as almost everyone around him, with suspicion and hostility.

Sherry was stunned. She had lived through 9/11 with him, and she thought that their shared experience would only serve to bond them closer, not tear them apart. She might have known how to handle it if he had become hyperemotional or anxious; those reactions would have made sense to her. Yet she didn't know what to do with this angry, sullen man.

Post-Traumatic Stress Disorder

There is a three-symptom cluster that determines if a person has succumbed to post-traumatic stress disorder (PTSD), as listed in *Diagnostic and Statistical Manual of Mental Disorders DSM IV*:

- Re-experiencing symptoms (intrusive thoughts, nightmares, etc.)
- Avoidance and numbing (inability to feel love and joy)
- Hypervigilance (the state of constantly being on the alert for danger)

In "Your Brain, Mindful Presence and Five Practices to Energize Love in Your Relationship," Athena Staik lists three common patterns connected to the high levels of distress a person suffers from in post-traumatic stress disorder:

1. Hyperaroused, fearful, anxious, irritable, and aggressive. Each partner is easily triggered by the other—especially if the non-traumatized person is unaware of what her partner is suffering.
2. Distant, withdrawn, emotionally numb.
3. Highly emotional in response to the one who is withdrawn. The emotional partner increases distress by becoming more frustrated causing the withdrawn one to move inward even more.

What Sherry didn't realize was that Adam wasn't just dealing with his feelings about 9/11. The anniversary had simply burst open the dam he had built to block other emotions he'd been holding back for years. Adam had formed a disorganized attachment style as a result of growing up in a violent family. He would regularly watch his drunken father beat his mother until he passed out. He left home as soon as he could, at the age of seventeen, but he took a job in a maximum security prison. There couldn't have been a worse place for a boy to work who had already decided that men were mean, selfish, and treacherous. There he bore witness to more violence and disheartening displays of the ugly side of human nature.

Thanks to his attachment style, he craved security but had difficulty trusting anyone. The World Trade Center bombings had merely cemented his belief that human beings were treacherous. Until 9/11, however, Sherry had never known any trauma. She had grown up securely attached in a loving home, surrounded by a mellow, stable network of parents, siblings, and extended family.

Sherry hadn't seen what Adam had seen; she couldn't comprehend just how much evil there was in the world, he thought. She couldn't possibly understand his feelings. And in some ways he was right. The anniversary really was affecting him more intensely than Sherry because it was causing him to re-experience his old trauma in addition to the new one. But Sherry thought he was being overly dramatic. She'd suffered on 9/11, too, and she wasn't walking around making everyone miserable. What's more, her parents were Holocaust survivors. Now there were two people who understood suffering, yet they had raised her to believe in love, hope, and optimism. What was Adam's problem?

As Adam felt more and more that Sherry was incapable of understanding or supporting him, he started to withdraw from her sexually. Their marriage had almost disintegrated by the time they made their way to a therapist's office.

Five Steps for Renegotiating Through Trauma

Ultimately, renegotiating with your spouse hinges on accepting that his perception of reality can be dramatically different from yours based on how past experiences have taught him to interpret the world. To work through this, couples must:

Accept Differences

We may think we are open-minded, but very often we go through life assuming that everyone is experiencing the world just as we are. When dealing with a traumatized loved one, that assumption has to be dropped. You have to learn to respect your dissimilarities and accept that the world will always look different to them than it does to you.

Offer the Care Your Spouse Needs, Not the Kind You Want to Give

What comforts you may not be what comforts your spouse. Sherry's contract with herself and her family had always been that one must go through life with a stiff upper lip. She had to renegotiate with herself that that approach simply wouldn't work for everyone, especially her husband.

Practice Compassion

Try to remember that no matter how irrational or incomprehensible, whatever your partner is feeling is very real. One's experience of reality is subjective, not objective; your connection to your spouse will be limited if you cannot find a way to step outside of yourself and try to see things from his or her perspective. If you can develop a strong sense of empathy (putting yourself in the other person's shoes), your capacity for compassion will multiply significantly, and your chances of improving your relationship will increase as well.

Create a Safe Environment

Offer a gentle touch, a warm hand, and physical contact whenever possible. The traumatized partner needs to renegotiate his perspective that the world is not a safe place, and his spouse can do that by simply being a nonjudgmental presence whenever he wakes up screaming, or feels anxious, or exhibits any other traumatic symptoms. If you are the partner of a traumatized spouse, becoming a source of comfort should give you a sense of gratification. In addition, when he finally turns to you, he will be showing you that he needs you, which feels good.

Go One Day at a Time

If you are trying to recover from trauma, all you can do is work on your feelings of safety every day. Test yourself and take small steps, one at a time, toward trusting your spouse more. If you suffer from anxiety, practice a mantra that might say, "I trust my wife/ husband," to help you remember that distrust is merely your way of transferring your emotions onto the person closest to you. In this way you can renegotiate your image of your spouse as a threat to one of support and comfort. In addition, you might set up small challenges to accomplish with your spouse, such as a 5K run or even just a boat ride across the lake. When you turn to see that your spouse hasn't left your side, it will help you feel more secure.

When couples can work together to learn how to regulate their emotions, develop a joint understanding of how their past contributes to their feelings about the present, and form a secure, intimate attachment, their marriage will thrive.

Chapter 15

Addiction: Recovering Your True Selves

Even when only one member of a couple is an addict, both members can contribute to sustaining or ending the dependence. By default the addicted partner's recovery will change your perception of the relationship and of your spouse, and will also demand behavioral changes from you. It will likely require that you acknowledge the damage the addiction has done to your relationship, and probably demand forgiveness from the addict as well. As sex-addiction expert Patrick Carnes writes in *Don't Call It Love*, regaining trust, setting limits, and keeping the communication channels open are all part and parcel of healing your relationship following sobriety. Most of all, however, it's about renegotiating your boundaries.

The Starting Point

Many people probably think that it's easy to tell when an addiction to pleasure, food, or mood-enhancing substances has created a barrier between two people, but it can actually be a very subtle process. The rift is often not appreciated until you realize that you are no longer making free choices, either because you are enslaved to the addiction or because you are imprisoned in your role as the addict's enabler. Either way, in order for you to have come this far, you had to have believed that your behavior was acceptable. Now it's time to break that agreement. Once you're ready, what happens next depends on whether you are the addict, or the spouse of an addict. It is a rare person who can simply walk away from an addiction through ferocious self-negotiation and free will, though it can be done. More likely, an addict should ride the momentum of his decision and check himself into a rehabilitation facility as quickly as possible. For the spouse, however, there are some negotiations that need to be made right away.

Negotiating Your Boundaries

At this point, how your spouse will feel about your decision to break your implicit contract as an enabler is irrelevant. The only bargain you need to make is with yourself, and it should be, "I'm done." When you can say that with conviction, think about what your new boundaries are and what you will and will not accept.

Getting Help

Sometimes the first step in your renegotiation with yourself or your addicted spouse is to start therapy so that you never feel like you are working all alone. Al-Anon, the Alcoholics Anonymous branch for relatives of addicted family members, is a helpful resource for learning how to love with detachment, as well as an excellent source of comfort and encouragement for you. Its theme of learning to love with detachment is probably valuable for many other aspects of relationships as well.

Renegotiate Your Role

Only once you have committed to that contract with yourself—"I'm done being an enabler"—should you approach your spouse and explain that you are renegotiating the bargain you struck together. The key is that when you do announce your plan, you remain personal and loving without being accusatory. You should be tender and calm, even in the face of what is likely to be an angry or pained reaction. Addicts are masters of denial.

Negotiation 101

One powerful negotiation tool you can try to use to help your partner see that his addiction is detrimental to his life is to encourage him to notice if he is neglecting anything that he values when his craving becomes his central focus. In this way, you are forcing him to compare his love for his addiction with something about which he reports to care. If you can gently help him see the truth, which is that everything around him is suffering from neglect, it may inspire him to accept your assistance in getting treatment.

Initiate Change with Influence, Not Control

Unlike many of the negotiations you will undertake in your lifetime, once you have explained to an addict the new points of your contract, there's not much left to be said. You can reiterate at every turn your love and support, but you will never convince your partner to get help with words. Only he can convince himself. What you can do is exert influence by showing how you plan to uphold your new contract through your actions. Al-Anon teaches addicts' family members that they need to learn to be supportive, but not compromise newly set boundaries. If that means changing the locks because you catch your spouse drinking beer in the basement after he swore he wouldn't touch another drop, so be it.

Once you've taken these steps to clarify the new parameters of what you will and will no longer tolerate, there's not much more you can do for the moment. Only when the addict has begun the path toward sobriety can the next renegotiation stage begin.

Marion and Jim

Marion thought she had it all. She and her husband, Jim, had begun their relationship in the late nineties when the dot-com money was still rolling and so was all that it could buy. They met and remet at numerous cocaine-fueled parties before finally falling in love; after that they were inseparable—except for the occasional couples with whom they'd swap partners for the night.

For Marion, now married almost twelve years, ensconced in her suburban home, the mother of four children, and sober for a decade, the hedonism in which they indulged was almost impossible to fathom. Not that the road to respectability was easy. After a year or so of cocaine-dusted, sexually adventurous newlywed bliss, she had realized that she wanted children. This had been the incentive she needed to get on the road to sobriety and start urging Jim to get on it with her. She had tried going cold turkey, but in the end both she and Jim had had to join Narcotics Anonymous as well as a therapy group. It had been a brutal process for both of them, but looking over the heads of their children when they sat down to dinner, they both knew they were happier now than they'd ever been.

At least, that was what Marion thought until the day she got a phone call from a woman named Becky, who announced, "You should just let him go. I love him, and he loves me." When she confronted Jim, he admitted that over the years, while Marion had been keeping the children company as they fell asleep, and usually falling asleep herself, he had turned to the Internet and masturbated to pornography for lack of a better sex partner. After a while he starting calling the numbers. When he actually encountered these woman he realized that he could get the same high from the anticipation of meeting them that he used to feel when he was on cocaine.

Marion immediately demanded that they enter couple's therapy, and Jim readily agreed. It was almost a relief to have everything out in the open so he could get some help.

Some Contracts Need to Be Broken

Jim had to do a lot of work on his own to break the grip of his addiction. He eventually came to terms with the emotional incest he suffered as a child at the hands of his mother, a former *Vogue* model and alcoholic, who used her little boy as an emotional stand-in after his father passed away when he was five years old. The behavior didn't stop following remarriage, and in fact Jim's home life got worse as the new husband drank profusely and used a heavy hand on him. His had been a childhood of little closeness, inconsistent rules, and inadequate supervision. Jim always loved Marion and his children with all his heart, but through therapy he realized that in looking for sex with anonymous women he was seeking to eradicate the sense of powerlessness that his mother instilled in him.

Once aware of this information, over a period of several years, Jim was able to break the contract he'd forged as a child with his mother—that he was powerless—and renegotiate one with his wife that said: I don't need to use sex to prove myself.

Negotiating as a Couple While the Addict Heals

In tandem with Jim's individual recovery effort, Jim and Marion would need to renegotiate all of the terms, boundaries, and rules of their marriage to make sure that wherever Jim turned, he felt supported and loved. This would help deter his cravings and limit the triggers that used to send him into a binge spiral.

Remember Your Strengths as a Couple

Remind each other of your strengths as a couple, and why your marriage is worth fighting for. Marion and Jim's list included things like, "We counterbalance each other well; when one of us freaks out, the other stays calm," "We back each other up in front of the children," and "We still enjoy sleeping together."

Schedule Times to Talk

This may be the most powerful negotiating move you can do. It's not enough to promise to talk more—you need to build it into your week. Maybe you decide that every Wednesday evening your wife will pick up some dessert on her way home from work, and you will spend an hour together after dinner, no exceptions. The point is to encourage as much togetherness as possible to stimulate the production of oxytocin, the bonding hormone. You can speak about each other's frustrations, or about cravings, or not. Do converse about the times when you choose your partner over your craving, or when you feel like your boundaries have been violated. You can discuss the good and the bad; just keep much of your thoughts and feelings in full view. Marion and Jim arranged a standing appointment with a babysitter, and every week they had a date away from the house. They would use their time together to check in and talk about Jim's progress and Marion's feelings, but they'd also just try to enjoy being in each other's company, and remembering not only why they loved each other, but why they liked each other.

They also agreed to take a half-hour walk together every morning. What better way to start your day than with a little exercise with the person you love? They usually used this time to chat about any issues regarding the children.

Measure the Five Elements for Relationship Fulfillment

This exercise is a good way to end your scheduled "catch up" time. For a few months, upon returning home Marion and Jim would refer to a checklist of the five fulfillment elements, as listed in *Don't Call It Love*:

1. Offering and welcoming intimacy
2. Exhibiting resilience
3. Giving and receiving pleasure
4. Showing positive feelings
5. Handling disappointment and change with grace

First, they would evaluate themselves on how well they thought they were acting on these ideals. Then they would switch lists and evaluate each other. Whenever there was a discrepancy between what one partner thought he was giving and what the other partner felt she was receiving or witnessing, the two would discuss the matter to see what improvements could be made.

Re-establish Trust in Yourselves and in Each Other

Be honest about your past, and about your fears. Reveal your vulnerabilities, and be kind when your spouse exposes his or hers. Let your partner know about any pain you suffered as a child. It will only make her love you more.

Decide What Is Acceptable and What Is Off-Limits

Off-limits is any action that builds a wall or a barrier (as opposed to a boundary or a picket fence, which is essential) between you and your partner. Whatever you can't tell her, whatever makes you feel too much shame, is probably off-limits.

Renegotiating your relationship when one or both of you are recovering from an addiction is a long, arduous process, one that you will have to commit to for the rest of your life together. There will always be the possibility that an unexpected trigger or temptation could lead a recovering addict astray, but the chances of relapse are lower in individuals whose families participate in their recovery, and especially in those whose families readjust their dynamics and habits to accommodate the addict's efforts. That means that when the whole family lives in a way that supports the addict's requirements, chances for sobriety increase. When an alcoholic opens a cupboard in the kitchen and finds a bottle of whiskey or a food addict lives in a home filled with junk food this does not signal we are in this together.

Every couple has to work to preserve a bond that is strong enough to endure life's challenges together. As each partner develops a strong sense of who they are, heals from childhood trauma, and takes responsibility for personal recovery, they are then able to offer important contributions to the relationship and the family.

Chapter 16

Spiritual Quests: Searching for Meaning Without Losing Each Other

It was not very long ago that people's religious affiliation dictated many aspects of their lives, from whom their community said they could marry to what jobs they could hold. While America is still far more religious than many other Western countries, overall faith has lost much of its central authority. Evidence of religion's weakened power can be seen in the decreasing rates of marriage. A recent Brookings Institution study found that, whereas in 1950 married couples represented 78 percent of American households, in 2010 it was only 48 percent. In addition, we see more unmarried partners with children and more couples who choose to cohabitate. Though we may be a less formally religious country, we are still a highly spiritual one. An August 2010 survey of 1,200 eighteen- to twenty-nine-year-olds, sponsored by LifeWay Christian Resources, found that 78 percent of generation Y, those born between the years of 1981 and 2000 (the first cohort to come of age in the new millennium), consider themselves more spiritual than religious.

Whether you consider yourself religious, spiritual, both, or neither, life can offer experiences that challenge you to rethink those beliefs. If this happens to you or your partner, it can take a surprising amount of renegotiation for your relationship to adjust. It's not until we change our views on something as important as our spiritual needs or religious affiliations—or lack thereof—that we realize how intrinsic they have become to our relationship.

Spiritual Beliefs Matter

Studies have indicated that partners who share religious beliefs have greater marital stability and fewer conflicts than couples who don't.

Religion Matters

Couples that share an aversion to all religion don't report more conflict or unhappiness, but they do lack the structures that religion provides that help support marriage through tough times.

This research explains the spiritual renegotiation Dennis and Kathleen were forced to embark upon. At the time, they had been married for twenty years. Though they loved each other very much, their radically different religious beliefs had caused a great deal of friction over those years. Until she met and fell in love with Dennis, Kathleen had always thought she would marry a devout Catholic like herself.

Dennis, however, was an ex-Catholic and wanted nothing to do with organized religion. He believed that formal religion filled people's heads with superstitions, fear, and self-consciousness, especially with regard to sex. Still, he respected her beliefs, and Kathleen had never loved a man the way she loved Dennis. She was sure that once they had children he would find his way back to the Church.

That didn't happen. Dennis didn't mind if Kathleen attended church and participated in religious events on her own, but he resisted when she tried to introduce their children into the Catholic community. In fact, every time each of their seven children prepared for another Catholic milestone, tensions in their home would rise. Dennis never stood in the way of Kathleen's insistence on raising the children according to her faith, but often he punished her with passive-aggressive silence.

Once the children's religious education was complete, the foundation of Dennis and Kathleen conflicts disappeared, but without that constant source of head butting, they found that they weren't talking much at all. They only discovered a way to reconnect once Dennis realized that he felt lost and started searching for something to help give his life meaning now that he didn't have children to raise. On a whim, he began to study qigong—a Chinese martial art with a heavy element of philosophy and spiritualism—and, much to his surprise, liked it. In fact, he started practicing every day. At first Kathleen dismissed his interest as a fad, but as he became more and more involved in it, attending retreats and workshops, she began to feel threatened. This man had ridiculed her for twenty years for her Catholicism, and now he was joining a bunch of strangers in the park every day to move and spin like the Karate Kid in slow motion?

Give Your Spouse Space

If you are uncomfortable with your spouse's new or always spiritual interest, or he seems uncomfortable with yours, remember that developing a spiritual consciousness also facilitates more self-love as we begin to appreciate our gifts and feel secure about our place in the world. This stimulates a greater ability to love others. If you can renegotiate your fixed idea of whom your spouse should be, you may be surprised to see how much more committed you will feel towards him because of his increased show of affection, compassion, and concern, even if you're not crazy about his new pursuit. When Dennis connected with his sacred needs, he in turn had more to give Kathleen. It took several months before Kathleen could admit that she liked the newer, more open-minded Dennis. Once she saw that he was earnestly searching for a path he could believe in, one that would give him the sense of peace and security that her Catholicism brought her, she was able to forgive him for fighting her efforts to pass on her beliefs to the children.

Participate

To show him her support, she asked if she could join him in the park one day. Dennis, who now had a better understanding of how hard it must have been for Kathleen to deal with his negativity toward her religion, readily accepted. They started taking walks in the evening and then doing qigong together at the local park. It wasn't Kathleen's favorite thing to do, but it was time spent with Dennis, and that was what really mattered.

One day as she was grabbing her keys to go to church, Dennis came out of the bedroom wearing pressed slacks and an Oxford shirt.

"Why are you dressed up?" she asked.

"I thought I'd come with you," Dennis replied.

With that, their relationship entered a blissful new phase. Renegotiating their feelings about the other's spiritual needs and practices allowed them to achieve the balance, open-mindedness, and flexibility that an ever-happy, fulfilling marriage thrives upon. Kathleen continues to practice qigong with Dennis, and Dennis sometimes accompanies Kathleen to church. Often their pew is filled with some of their children and grandchildren. On these days, Kathleen has everyone over to the house for Sunday lunch. Last

Sunday lunch Dennis looked at his wife and family and realized he has never felt so content in his life.

Whether it's through religion, meditation, martial arts, yoga, or any other practice, actively taking steps toward spiritual fulfillment adds depth, peacefulness, and love to everyday existence.

Chapter 17

Illness: Finding Intimacy When You're Feeling Lousy

For some people, there's a silver lining to being laid up by a short illness, like bronchitis, the flu, or even a broken arm or tonsillectomy—for a short, precious time, they get to be coddled and comforted, no strings attached. Not everyone relishes this kind of attention, of course—you might call them "difficult patients"—but for those who do, it can be an unexpected opportunity for bonding with their partner.

When the illness drags on, though, or becomes permanent or debilitating, the caretaker can start to chafe at the pressure and responsibility, and the patient might struggle with bitterness, fear, and self-loathing. They may have meant it when they promised to love in sickness and in health, but no one ever wants to imagine their future could hold such a scenario. In times such as these, it's crucial to find ways to build intimacy so that the couple doesn't become overwhelmed by the illness and forget to keep working on cherishing their marriage.

Sustaining the Health of Your Relationship

Life can be cruel and throw unexpected illness at us. But even if luck goes your way, the laws of nature predict that at some point toward the later years of your relationship, one or both of you will need caretaking on some level. Given that inevitability, it's a good idea to develop a preemptive strategy to help make that occasion of life as loving, sensual, and bonded as the healthy times.

For example, thinking ahead while you are young and vigorous about how you want to spend your golden years will help sustain you for your entire marriage. Empty nesters, especially, would benefit from planning ahead. No one really wants to leave the family home, but wouldn't it be better to make arrangements ahead of time, before illness forces you to? Downsizing or moving to a community with built-in amenities for older people would mean that when that time in your life arrives, there's no thinking or planning to be done, making the transition and negotiation far less stressful.

Three Must-Haves to a Fulfilling Relationship

If you or your partner is struggling with chronic or debilitating injury, it's incredibly easy to focus exclusively on the health of the patient and neglect the health of your relationship. Do not fall into this trap. It is imperative that you check in with each other often to see whether you are each receiving the three must-haves to a satisfying relationship: emotional closeness, mutual concern, and sexual creativity. Let's look at each of these in turn.

Emotional Closeness

Sometimes illness brings a couple closer together because it allows them to demonstrate their need for each other. The ill person is vulnerable; what does the healthy person realize? What life without the partner could be? But you don't have to wait for tragedy to strike to begin fueling these feelings. Build your emotional closeness ahead of time and it will carry you through any illness you may have to face together. It's important that you enjoy your moments of togetherness no matter what the circumstance.

Mutual Concern

This is the ability to remember that two people are in the relationship, not just the sick one. Clearly, when someone we love is sick or hurt, we're compelled to do whatever we can to ease his or her pain. We show our love and concern in the tender way we bring food, or wash his body, or read to her when she's tired, or tend to daily needs. But it's very common for the partner who dons the role of caretaker to become so involved that he loses himself in it. Sometimes people drive their own health into the ground, so devoted are they and determined not to let their spouses feel abandoned, alone, or neglected. The patient, then, must make sure to remember to acknowledge the other person's emotions. Reminisce about the scary times, the interesting times, the sexy times, the awe-inspiring times. Speak about your family and your friends. Tell each other the news. Keep the line of communication open to the world not just to the bedside. Show an interest in your caretaker's day, encourage him or her to go out and bring back engaging stories. Make it clear that you want him to feel fine as much as he wants you to.

Sexual Creativity

When you're feeling lousy often the last thing in the world you want is sex. And when faced with a bedridden, broken, or sick spouse, sex can seem like a selfish idea, or even distasteful. But even if sex is no longer possible, or you feel too miserable to try, you can still find gentle, loving, creative ways to renew your sexual life. Tease each other, touch each other lightly, flirt. Do what you can. Even if you don't want sex, it feels good to feel someone else's touch and know they still find you attractive.

Stella and Seymour

Adapting to the loss of the sexual component of your life does not mean giving up sex forever; rather, it means renegotiating your definition of sex. Intimacy does not have to equal intercourse, as Stella and Seymour discovered. Both widowed, they liked each other immediately upon meeting. Seymour, however, was more enthralled than Stella. He was a kind, intelligent, attractive physician, but he was impotent. Now that Stella was ready to have a new relationship, she was also ready to start having sex again. She couldn't imagine a future with a man who couldn't get an erection. But she continued to date Seymour, and quickly discovered that in the right hands, a woman didn't need intercourse to have some of the best sex of her life.

There are five components of sexuality that Seymour intuitively understood:

1. Sensuality. We feel sexy when we're able to indulge in our senses and our appetites. Sensuality requires a strong awareness of our body and an appreciation for how we can use our five senses to heighten our sense of pleasure. For example, Seymour went to a department store's perfume department one day and asked the saleswomen to show him scents that smelled like lilacs. This is his and Stella's favorite floral scent. One in particular smelled exactly like Stella to him. He bought it and gave it to her on the anniversary of their first sexual encounter. She flipped. Now whenever they are ready for bed Stella dabs a little all over, and they're both in seventh heaven.

2. Intimacy. As we've established, when we touch, cuddle, kiss, or simply hold hands, we release the bonding hormone oxytocin, which heightens our ability to experience emotional closeness as well as return that closeness in kind. We also release dopamine, a feel-good brain chemical that can have a similar impact on the mind as drugs do. Seymour never passed up an

opportunity to touch Stella, whether they were having dinner with friends or alone in the car together.

3. Identity. The more we develop a clear sense of who we are and cultivate clear personal boundaries, the less we are afraid to merge our identity with another. Lack of fear makes us less inhibited and open to surrendering to our sensual and sexual pleasures. This is a feedback loop that exists no matter if we are sick or healthy.

4. Reproduction. The possibility of reproduction and child rearing wasn't an issue for Stella and Seymour but it can be a big part of what draws a couple together and gives them incentive to surrender to sex.

5. Sexualization. The use of sexuality to influence others could sound like a negative, but it depends on one's goal. Seymour used his sexuality to influence the person he loved, but the outcome shows that it was for the best. It is about influencing one another to create a better life outcome than either could achieve on his own.

A Positive Attitude Helps

How did Seymour intuit these five components? They had become integrated, a part of his drive for life, thanks to the positive and supportive influence of his parents during his childhood and a natural ability to see obstacles as challenges over which he should try to rise. It was that attitude that had allowed him to cope with his first wife's slow death from heart disease at the age of fifty-eight.

So when he recovered from the prostate operation that robbed him of his ability to maintain erections, he was disappointed and sad but it didn't bog him down. Rather, he determined that his next challenge would be to become more creative in expressing himself sexually. And lucky for Stella, he did. He found so many ways to give her an orgasm she felt like a teenager again.

Stella Renegotiates with Herself

Stella had decided that intercourse was necessary for her to feel sexually fulfilled. By renegotiating that assumption in favor of the idea that sexual fulfillment can be sustained through intimacy, compassion, kindness, and a shared enthusiasm for life, she was able to appreciate Seymour's great qualities and allow herself to fall in love.

Another way to restart your sex life when one of you is physically incapacitated is to broaden your definition of sexuality to mean any activity that is mutually stimulating and pleasurable. This opens up countless opportunities to experience the same benefits of open communication and closeness that sex provides.

Tracy and Caleb

Tracy has fought breast cancer for five years. She finally had a double mastectomy at the urging of her doctor and her husband although she needed only one breast removed.

Tracy and her husband Caleb had to undergo several renegotiations:

Their Self-Image as Healthy People

For a while Tracy would look in the mirror and not feel like she was a whole woman. But as time passed and she learned to accept the events of the past five years, she also learned to appreciate her reconstructed breasts. Doing so helped her reconnect with her sensual side and she was ready to start having sex again.

Their Sexuality

It had been a long time since Tracy and Caleb had had sex. Caleb used to initiate, but he had not since the surgery. Tracy assumed it was because he was turned off by her new body, or just scared to touch her again. But as it turned out, her assumption was incorrect;

she was merely projecting her self-loathing onto him. After talking to Caleb about her feelings, she found out that Caleb was anxious to make love to her, but he was waiting for her to initiate. He was nervous, too, and her initiation would help him get over that. What a surprise for Tracy! For the first forty years of their marriage they'd had an implicit contract that Caleb would initiate and Tracy would decide whether they would make love or not. Tracy was intrigued by her renegotiated role assignment in the lovemaking department and worked on incorporating this into their new deal.

Their Concept of Their Own Mortality

Tracy's brush with death made her appreciation for life ten times greater than it was before she was sick. While she can't say she's glad she got cancer, she acknowledges the opportunities it has brought her and recognizes how lucky she is to have been able to see how many people care so deeply about her. Caleb has had a harder time accepting how close he came to losing her, and in addition, is struggling with fears about his own health. Whereas once he felt invincible, he can no longer deny the reality of death and he finds himself scared of it. He talks about his fears with his wife, though, and there is no one who understands his feelings better.

Maricella and Richie

These three negotiation points, among others, also provided a framework for Maricella and Richie as they worked to save their twenty-year marriage following the terrible accident that kept Richie in rehab for a year and left him paralyzed from the waist down and wheelchair bound. They had been a strong, in-sync couple before the accident, reveling in the renewed love affair and sex life they were enjoying in their empty nest, and relishing their time to pursue new adventures together. The accident changed all that, though. Richie hated being in a wheelchair and felt depressed and emasculated. Maricella was exhausted and frustrated. At forty-nine, she could not imagine never making love again for the rest of her life with Richie. Richie, too, though physically incapable of sexual intercourse, mourned his sexual identity. Both felt that their sexuality was a major component of who they were, and neither was ready to let that part die.

They needed to accept that they could no longer be the couple they once were, and find things to cherish about the couple that they could now become. Both people are physical beings and denying that part of themselves would mean that they were willfully amputating an essential gift of their humanness. For many, only when they get cancer, or lose an arm or leg, do they then realize how lucky they are to be alive. Ironically illness can add to life's pleasure because it is almost impossible to take for granted the normality of everyday life the way many of us do before tragedy strikes.

To give themselves over to gratitude for being alive and together, Maricella and Richie would have to focus on two important aspects of their new lives that are often overlooked: the welfare of the caregiver and the couple's sexuality.

Renegotiate Your Renegotiation

Sometimes we so successfully renegotiate our expectations of ourselves that they consume us. Maricella had accepted the sacrifices she would have to make in order to care for Richie. Now she needed to renegotiate again, because the new role she'd adopted as Richie's caretaker was threatening to overshadow her role as Richie's wife. She could no longer allow her role as "caretaker" to define her if she wanted to recreate a sensual, sexual life with her husband.

With Richie's blessing, she began to make an effort to get out. She took up knitting. She made new friends. She tried, as best she could, to continue the active, stimulating life she had been living before Richie's accident. In order to make sure Richie felt included, she'd return from all of her outings and share what she'd learned, stories of whom she'd met, and what she'd seen in great detail. When she discovered somewhere she knew Richie would enjoy, she'd make arrangements to take him there so he could see it, too. Concerts, movies, plays, restaurants—she scouted out everything and brought Richie to as many places that were wheelchair accessible as she could. She also discovered poker, and urged Richie to become her partner, which he did reluctantly at first, then enthusiastically as they both fell in love with the game and the social opportunity it provided.

Richie, for his part, finally decided that he needed to become more independent. He hired a nurse to come in three times a week to teach him how to handle his personal care, limiting Maricella to small tasks like helping him to shower, shave, and dress. He also became playful in these activities and soon the shower was transformed into their own spa retreat. In this way, he was able to stop thinking of Maricella as his nursemaid and remember that she was still his wife and lover.

Both Maricella and Richie had to make some major renegotiations with themselves.

Maricella had to renegotiate her role as caretaker and remember that:

1. She is entitled to live autonomous of Richie as she had before his accident.
2. She must encourage couple friendships as well as independent friendships.
3. It's not a sign of weakness to seek out advice from other caregivers or go to therapy.

Richie had to learn to accept that:

1. This experience is now a part of his life.
2. There has to be something positive to be found in what he is experiencing.
3. Maricella needs her husband back, and he should therefore make every effort to be the fun-loving man she married.
4. He will sometimes be afraid, but Maricella is there to talk to him, as are many other people within the community.
5. It is a joy to be alive each day.

By acknowledging these truths, couples can renegotiate their view of illness and disabilities. Instead of feeling sorry for themselves, they can look for the opportunities to strengthen their love for life and for each other.

Chapter 18

Death and Dying: Learning to Live with Loss

Renegotiation can save, heal, and boost any marriage through just about anything life can throw at it. Death, of course, is the exception—the only original contract that we cannot renegotiate with our partner for being together in the next stage—yet it is as much a part of life as living and loving. The best we can do when death approaches, assuming it gives us a little advance warning, is fight as hard as we can to live well together with the time we have left, as you saw in the previous chapters.

Yet as with everything in life, when one door closes, another one opens. While death robs us of further opportunities to renegotiate with our spouse, it is often in the aftermath that we can find a unique opportunity to renegotiate with ourselves and lay the groundwork for a future filled with happiness, hope, and love. As a wise person who lost two husbands once said, "There is life after death."

If You Are Dying

The best thing you can do for the people you love is to die a good death. Bless them, give them permission to go on, make sure they feel appreciated and loved. Use whatever energy you have left to think of something special to say about each of your loved ones, especially your life partner, and share those thoughts with them. If possible, put them in writing so your words will last forever. The great medieval poet Samuel the Prince put it succinctly in his poem:

> *Take heart in time of sorrow*
> *Though you face death's door.*
> *The candle flares before it dies,*
> *And wounded lions roar.*

Make sure your last roar offers a lifetime of meaning to those you leave behind.

If you are afraid of death, it's possible that you have lost touch with one or more of the three coping mechanisms we humans have developed to deal with the knowledge of our own death:

1. Living in the present—experience each moment to the fullest.
2. Identifying with institutions, such as church or country—your legacy lives on through your contributions.
3. Believing in the soul—in *Soul Dust*, Nicholas Humphrey suggests humans developed the concept of an eternal soul in order to avoid feeling that life and death is futile, since we are only here on earth a short time.

If you struggle with any of these concepts, working to renegotiate your feelings or beliefs about the legacy you want to leave behind will go a long way towards helping you find peace and fulfillment.

If Your Spouse Dies

There is very little to say about renegotiating with yourself after the death of your spouse. Of course you will have to decide what pacts to make with yourself now that you're single, how you want to live and where, for example. But most important is to decide to live well. We can all point to people who survive their spouses and go on to live active, happy lives—the ninety-year-old who still plays piano, the eighty-five-year-old who still dances the polka, the couple who gets married at the retirement home. What is their common link? Their lack of fear. When we no longer dread death, we release ourselves from a source of anxiety and leave more room for risk taking and new experiences.

So fear is the biggest renegotiation you can have with yourself now, before you are forced to confront death: Death is not something to be feared. It is merely the incentive we have to make sure that we live every precious drop of life we have to the fullest.

Gratitude for the gift of life is the most potent antidote to fear of death. Engaging in a spiritual practice can help to tune into feeling thankful. Enjoy the present; it is a gift that keeps on giving.

Good luck with your renegotiation project. I am happy to hear about your progress.

Get in touch through *drbonniejacobson@aol.com*.

Appendix

Resources

Ainsworth, Mary Salter, Mary C. Blehar, Everett Waters, and Sally Wall. *Patterns of Attachment: A Psychological Study of the Strange Situation.* Hillsdale, N. J.: Erlbaum, 1978.

American Psychiatric Association. *Diagnostic and Statistical Manual of Mental Disorders (DSM-IV)*, 1994. Arlington, VA: American Psychiatric Publishing, Inc.

American Psychological Association. "Stressed in America." Harris Interactive Survey. *Monitor on Psychology* 42, no. 1 (January 2011): 60.

Barry, Patricia. *Mental Health and Mental Illness*, 7th ed. New York: Lippincott, 2002.

Blackwell, Debra and Daniel Lichter. "Homogamy Among Dating, Cohabiting, and Married Couples." *The Sociological Quarterly* 45 (2004): 719–737.

Bowlby, John. "The Making and Breaking of Affectional Bonds." *British Journal of Psychiatry* 130 (1977): 201–210.

Carey, Benedict. "The Psychology of Cheating." *New York Times*, April 17, 2011.

Carnes, Patrick. *Don't Call It Love: Recovery From Sexual Addiction*. New York: Bantam, 1999.

_____. *Out of the Shadows: Understanding Sexual Addiction*, 3rd ed. City Center, Minnesota: Hazelden, 2001.

Chang, Althea. Special to the Street.com. "Couples and Money." Lawyer.com. April 2011.

Chapman, Gary. *The 5 Love Languages: The Secret to Love that Lasts*. Chicago: Northfield Publishing, 1992.

Diamond, Ronny, Mimi Meyers, David Kezur, Constance N. Scharf, and Margot Weinshel. *Couple Therapy for Infertility*. New York: Guilford Press, 1999.

Fisch, Joan. "Couple Therapy with Survivors of Childhood Trauma." *California Society for Clinical Social Work* 36, no. 1 (2010): 1, 8–10.

Fisher, Helen. *Why We Love*. New York: Henry Holt, 2004.

Fisher, Roger, William Ury, and Bruce Patton. *Getting to Yes*. New York: Penguin, 1991.

Gilbert, Daniel. *Stumbling on Happiness*. New York: Alfred A. Knopf, 2006.

Glahn, Sandra and William Cutrer. *When Empty Arms Become a Heavy Burden*. Grand Rapids: Kregel, 2010.

Grossman, Cathy Lynn. "72% of Millennials More Spiritual Than Religious." USA Today.com, October 14, 2010.

Humphrey, Nicholas. *Soul Dust: The Magic of Consciousness*. New Jersey: Princeton University Press, 2011.

Johnson, Susan M. and Lyn Williams-Keeler. "Couples Dealing with Trauma: The Use of Emotionally Focused Marital Therapy." *Journal of Marriage and Family Therapy* 24, no. 1 (January 1998): 25–40.

Kossek, E. Ernst and Cynthia Ozeki. "Work–Family Conflict, Policies, and the Job–Life Satisfaction Relationship: A Review and Directions for Organizational Behavior–Human Resources Research." *Journal of Applied Psychology* 83, no. 2 (1998): 139–149.

Margolis, Rachel and Mikko Myrskylä. "A Global Perspective on Happiness and Fertility." *Population and Development Review* 37 (2011): 29–56.

Miron-Spektor, Ella, Dorit Efrat-Treister, Anat Rafaeli, and Orin Schwarz-Cohen. "Others' Anger Makes People Work Harder Not Smarter: The Effect of Observing Anger and Sarcasm on Creative and Analytic Thinking." *Journal of Applied Psychology* (May 2011).

Myers, David G. *Psychology: Eighth Edition in Modules.* New York: Worth Publishers, 2006.

Nowak, Martin A. and Roger Highfield. *SuperCooperators: Altruism, Evolution, and Why We Need Each Other to Succeed.* New York: Free Press, 2011.

Ortega, Suzanne T., Hugh Whitt, and J. Allen Williams Jr. "Religious Homogamy and Marital Happiness." *Journal of Family Issues* 9 (1988): 224–239.

Peetz, Johanna and Lara Kammrath. "Only Because I Love You: Why People Make and Why They Break Promises in Romantic Relationships." *Journal of Personality and Social Psychology* 100, no. 5 (2011): 887–904.

Perlick, Deborah A., et al. "Multifamily Group Treatment for Veterans with Traumatic Brain Injury." *Professional Psychology: Research and Practice* 42, no. 1 (2011): 70–78.

Phillips, Suzanne and Dianne Kane. *Healing Together: A Couple's Guide to Coping with Trauma and Post-traumatic Stress*. Oakland: New Harbinger Publications, 2011.

Rogers, Carl *On Becoming a Person: A Therapist's View of Psychotherapy*. London: Constable, 1961.

Rusbult, Caryl E., Eli J. Finkel, and Madoka Kumashiro. "The Michelangelo Phenomenon." *Current Directions in Psychological Science* 18 (2009): 305–309.

Sager, Clifford J. *Marriage Contracts and Couple Therapy: Hidden Forces in Intimate Relationships*. Lanham, MD: Jason Aronson Publishers, 1997.

Salamon, Maureen. "Oxytocin Solidifies Relationships." *Proceedings of the National Academy of Science*, (November 2005). *http://oxytocincentral.com/2011/02/oxytocin-solidifies-relationships-studies-show/#more-605*.

Savitsky, Kenneth, et al. "The Closeness-Communication Bias: Increased Egocentricism Among Friends Versus Strangers." *Journal of Experimental and Social Psychology* 47 (2011): 269–273.

Schneider, Jennifer P. "Rebuilding the Marriage During Recovery from Compulsive Sexual Behavior." *National Council on Family Relations* 38, no. 3 (July 1989): 288–294. *www.jstor.org/stable/585054*.

Schwartz, Christine R. "Pathways to Educational Homogamy in Marital and Cohabiting Unions." *Demography* 47, no. 3 (2010): 735–753.

Seelig, Tina. "Mastering the Art of Everyday Negotiations." Creativity Rulz blog. *Psychology Today*. August 2009.

Seligman, Martin. *Flourish: A Visionary New Understanding of Happiness*. New York: Simon and Schuster, 2011.

Siegel, Daniel J. *The Developing Mind: How Relationships and the Brain Interact to Shape Who We Are*. New York: Guilford Press, 1999.

Smith, Anthony, et al. "Sexual and Relationship Satisfaction Among Heterosexual Men and Women: the Importance of Desired Frequency of Sex." *Journal of Sex & Marital Therapy* 37 (2011): 104–105.

Staik, Athena. "Your Brain, Mindful Presence and Five Practices to Energize Love in Your Relationship." *Neuroscience & Relationships*, May 5, 2011.

Tsapelas, Irene, Arthur Aron, and Terri Orbuch. "Marital Boredom Now Predicts Less Satisfaction, Nine Years Later." *Psychological Science* 20, no. 5 (2009): 543–545.

Ury, William. *Getting Past No*. New York: Bantam, 1993.

VanderDrift, Laura E., Gary W. Lewandowski, Jr., and Christopher R. Agnew. "Reduced Self-Expansion in Current Romance and Interest in Relationship Alternatives." *Journal of Social and Personal Relationships* 28 (2011): 356–373.

Waite, Linda. "Marital Biography and Health at Midlife." *Journal of Health and Social Behavior* 50, no. 3 (2009): 344–358.

Wilson, Chris M. and Andrew J. Oswald. "How Does Marriage Affect Physical and Psychological Health? A Survey of the Longitudinal Evidence." Institute for the Study of Labor (IZA) Discussion Paper no. 1619 (2005).

Wolfers, Justin. "How Marriage Survives." Brookings Institution, (2010).

Index

Identity, sense of, 119–20, 193
Illness, 189–98
    caretaker role during, 189–91, 193–97
    healthy relationship and, 190–96
    positive attitude during, 193
    sexual creativity and, 191–93
Infertility concerns, 157–65
Infidelity, 61–77. *See also* Extramarital affairs
Interests, supporting, 135–45
Intimacy. *See also* Sex
    building, 43–45, 55–59, 66, 102, 181, 189
    emotional intimacy, 7, 190–93
    finding, 189–98
    physical intimacy, 3–18, 55–57

Job loss, 119–26. *See also* Career transitions
Journal of Experimental Social Psychology, 132
Journal of Personality and Social Psychology, 110
Journal of Sex & Marital Therapy, 13

Kama Sutra, 11
Kammrath, Lara, 110

Legacy, leaving, 200
Loss, coping with, 199–201
Love languages, 50–51

About the Author

Bonnie Jacobson, PhD, is a preeminent authority on relationships. She is the author of six books on the subject. She is an adjunct professor in the applied psychology department at New York University where she trains graduate students to work in the public schools with disadvantaged youth on relationship issues both individually and in classroom groups as a whole. She also works with psychology students from Yeshiva University, Hunter University, and the University of Gottenberg in Sweden.

For the past forty years, Dr. Jacobson has been treating individuals, couples, and families. Her most powerful medium for influencing change are the modern analytic psychotherapy groups that she runs within her private practice. They train people how to give and receive feedback that allows authentic connections and also help to heal the unfinished conflicts from one's original family.

She is a media expert and multiple times has been on *Oprah*, *Montel Williams*, *Donohue*, *Geraldo Rivera*, and most of the other talk shows as well as many national and local news and radio shows throughout the past four decades. She is also frequently interviewed for newspapers and magazines throughout the United States and the United Kingdom.

Dr. Jacobson is a member of American Psychological Association, American Group Psychotherapy, and Eastern Group Psychotherapy. She is a certified group therapist and certified by the State of New York as a clinical psychologist.

The titles of her other books, which are in continual use, are listed in order of publication.

Love Triangles: Seven Steps to Break the Secret Ties That Poison Love, Crown Publisher, 1991.

If Only You Would Listen: How to Stop Blaming His or Her Gender and Start Communicating with the One You Love, St. Martin's Press, 1995.

Re-issued as *Intimate Listening: Seven Steps to Connect to the Heart and Soul of the One You Love*, iUniverse, 2008.

The Shy Single: A Bold Guide to Dating for the Less-Than-Bold Dater, Rodale Press, 2004.

Choose to be Happily Married: How Everyday Decisions Can Lead to Lasting Love, Adams Media, 2010.

Save Your Marriage in Five Minutes a Day: Simple Daily Strategies to Transform Your Relationship, Adams Media, 2011.

In her personal life, she gets to practice all that she teaches and writes about as she is married and has both biological and stepsons, daughters-in-law, grandchildren, nieces and nephews, great-nieces and -nephews, and wonderful siblings and their spouses as well as intimate lifelong friends. The closer the relationships the more challenges they present, and this is what keeps her honest and humble.